Books by PATRICIA L. LINDSAY:

"It comes down to wanting something"- copyright 1994, Published- 2006*

DWELLERS ON TWO PLANES

Author Of- *It Comes Down to Wanting Something and Desert Queen*

PATRICIA LINDSAY

authorHOUSE

AuthorHouse™
1663 Liberty Drive
Bloomington, IN 47403
www.authorhouse.com
Phone: 833-262-8899

Published by AuthorHouse 09/28/2020

ISBN: 978-1-7283-7066-8 (sc)
ISBN: 978-1-7283-7238-9 (e)

Print information available on the last page.

Any people depicted in stock imagery provided by Getty Images are models, and such images are being used for illustrative purposes only. Certain stock imagery © Getty Images.

This book is printed on acid-free paper.

Because of the dynamic nature of the Internet, any web addresses or links contained in this book may have changed since publication and may no longer be valid. The views expressed in this work are solely those of the author and do not necessarily reflect the views of the publisher, and the publisher hereby disclaims any responsibility for them.

CONTENTS

DEDICATION

JAMES E. LINDSAY

1942-2005

Dedicated to my loving husband, Lindsay, who said:

"IF YOU KNOW NO BOUNDRIES

OF IMAGINATION AND ABILITIES,

YOU CAN ACCOMPLISH

ANYTHING!"

Amanuensis' Foreword

I never intended to write this book! However, one evening, about one year after my husband's death, while I was crying in my living room about the loss of James, my spiritual guide appeared in my mind's eye and *he appeared with scrolls in his hands and asked me to write with him*. I am a sensitive and have experienced hearing and feeling Spirit. I knew he was my spiritual guide because I had studied with Astara Brotherhood for over four years and graduated 8th degree metaphysics in 1994. I recognized the teacher. I had spent a lifetime respecting what I had gained from those incredible wisdom studies and can say that they made a tremendous difference for the better in my life.

The very next day I went into my computer room and meditated to a relaxed level and I began to hear his words clearly and concisely. His words came in amazingly fast. Typing rapidly - it was all I could do to keep up with him! We would write two or three pages quickly then that was it for the day. I would then go back over what was dictated, work on the punctuation of text and paragraph formations.

I had to break away from the writing when my wonderful younger brother Christopher became seriously ill, diagnosed with fourth stage melanoma cancer. I then spent my time traveling from my home in Tallassee, Alabama to Nashville, Tennessee; my brother Chris had been accepted into a major drug trial of a new drug seeking FDA approval. This drug was designed to treat late stage melanoma cancer. Vanderbilt University was the designated host medical facility conducting the drug trial. My older brother, Bill, would fly in from Philadelphia, Pa. to the Nashville airport with Chris.

DWELLERS ON TWO PLANES- Foreword continued:

It was a race against time trying to save Christopher's life. I would meet them at the Marriott Hotel off of Broadway Avenue, downtown Nashville and we would have wonderful family dinners together! The three of us made the best of it, no matter what! Prior to Nashville, I would drive to Bethesda, Maryland and see Chris whenever he went to the National Institute of Health for operations and other medical treatments-procedures trying to stop the cancer from spreading through his body. Bill would travel with Chris, faithfully at his side. We lost our brother in Oct. 2011 to cancer. He was 53 years old. The FDA has approved the drug, "Zelboraf!" The **"*In memoriam*"** in the front of this book has honored a great guy, **Christopher James Leahy.**

After several months of mourning the loss of Christopher, I came back into my computer room ***determined to finish the book!*** I have made a concerted effort all through these chapters to stay as close to what was dictated in the exact manner and word formation, sequentially. Mrs. Anderson, my editor, changed only points of grammar and other very basic elements, as necessary, respecting the context of what my teacher, Rama said ***exactly.***

As an author, I have written two other books which are available on my website, patricialindsaybooks.com. However, this is my first book of non-fiction, metaphysical intent; this is a channeled book. ***My task here was to bring teacher Rama's words to life*** and share them with the world. In doing that I hope that many will profit from his wise words on spiritual guidance into the Millennium and beyond.

With love to all of you,
Patricia L. Lindsay

In Memoriam

CHRISTOPHER JAMES LEAHY, SR.

1958-2011

My beautiful brother Chris! I will miss you forever!

The loss of you is too deep for tears.

We will always have Nashville, Tenn. All those trips to meet with you and our dearest brother Bill at Vanderbilt University; fighting to save your life through a drug trial, pioneering a new drug to fight melanoma, late stage cancer.

Today this drug has FDA approval. The drug is called "ZELBORAF" and I will always remember you, Chris, as a hero! The next patient with melanoma cancer and the cancer code cell marker that matches the drug will have an extension of life option against this deadly disease. This is possible today thanks to you and the other courageous participants in this drug trial that gave their very lives to advance this wonderful new drug!

WITH SPECIAL THANKS TO:

Deborah J. Anderson- Editor

Peter H. Heberer – Asst. Editor, Production Mgr.-

DISCLAIMER, OVERVIEW, PLEASE BE ADVISED:

That this book, Dwellers on Two Planes, is a metaphysical book. Metaphysics is the difficult branch of philosophy that deals with the first principles of things, including abstract concepts such as Being, Existence, Purpose, Universals, Property, Relation, Event, Knowing, Substance, Causality, Identity, Time, Space and many others. An example of a noted Philosopher who studied within this branch would be: Baruch Spinoza, a Dutch Philosopher of Portuguese Sephardi origin. One of the early thinkers of the Enlightenment and modern biblical criticism, including modern concepts of the self and the universe, he came to be considered one of the great rationalists of the 17th century philosophy. Born on November 24, 1632, Amsterdam, Netherlands, it is said that he influenced Gottfried Wilhelm Leibniz, Albert Einstein, Friedrich Nietzsche, George Wilhelm Fredrich Hegel. History reveals these thinkers were influenced by Rene Descartes, Plato, Aristotle, Thomas Hobbes, Francis Bacon, Niccolo Machiavelli, Epicurus and others.

The reader should know that this Spirit Guide, encompassed in this book, came to me through the process of meditation, a process which I would define as an art form requiring a considerable, deep level of concentration, and these meditation process sessions have delivered his words. I want to say also, that his opinions and statements are his and I may or may not agree with them in total or even in a limited manner. However, I believe in free speech and that he deserves his scribe to deliver his thoughts in entirety, except to make it readable within today's world and without prejudice to meaning, evaluation or nature of the content. All readers should know, and I would hope that they would be open to the datum, delivered on the pages, as this information is from a Spirit that is not living in a human body now on Planet Earth; in fact, he says his location is Astara Highlands Central, a location that is not on Planet Earth but beyond this planet. However, he said, when I heard him in meditation, that when he was in human form, he was from the order of Melchizedek, the original order of priests.

I consider this a great honor to have taken his notes, faithfully, and present them herein my book today. Here they are, teacher Rama's thoughts. As this entire book is about Planet Earth, its people and the universe around our planet, I hope that you will find his thoughts, as I find them- useful, wise, provoking and truly extraordinary.

Finally, I need to qualify my relationship with Astara, and say that I am not a paid employee, of Astara Brotherhood. However, I have graduated 8th degree with that fine, metaphysical, educational organization in 1994. I receive no financial compensation from their organization which, as I recall, was a 501 C in the State of California, at the time I graduated. This book is solely my production. I have not sought approval or disapproval from any organization regarding this book, other than my publisher, Authorhouse. My experience with this Spirit Guide has been profound and changed my life forever! I hope that you will connect with him as you read and feel his great love and concern for Planet Earth and all Earthians!

With love to all of you,
Patricia L. Lindsay

CHAPTER ONE

DIMENSIONS AND DISTINGUISHING CHARACTERISTICS OF LOVE

SO MOTE IT BE, we have begun this task again of writing with new lessons, information for Planet Earth from the realm of Astara, Highlands Central, well above the Earth's atmosphere, reachable through spirituality and that is what we speak of here today!

The Higher-Self is the spiritual guide for all of humanity. Connection to this part of each human mind makes the pace of life much easier and swifter to proceed with, in all respects.

Today, life is so rushed on Planet Earth. We see that there are many distractions and so much ill will and intent worldwide, that it is difficult to think of humanity as rising beyond this current round of evolution. However, that being stated, we wish to congratulate all souls that seek the higher path to the Godhead, to the wisdom head. It is *these aspiring souls that will walk with me, Master Rama.*

By way of introduction, I am a Master of the great ancient metaphysical mystery school, Astara. At Astara-Highlands Central, a location above the Earth, I am simply a loving teacher and enjoy partaking with students and imparting studies that are taught here daily. We in the Spirit are not dead to "doing"; it is just that the "doing" is entirely different than the Earth plane "doing".

To wit, we have no physical bodies of flesh. We have no need of physical food, such as the taking of breakfast or dinner. We have no attraction to gaining or acquiring physical wealth and power as over on your side. Here, we instantly create what we need, instantly, via thought; which thought is also instantly translating into the form of the thing we need. *This is the nature of Spirit manifesting here, on the Spirit- side.*

On your side, things are slowed by the reality of creation through physicality, an entirely different process, which requires time and skill. Although, even then, not all that is received was asked for. Some receive exactly what they ask for while others do not. Have you a desire to know how this process works? If you would listen then, I would like to take you through that door, that process *of attainment.*

First, there is the matter and measure of Karma and how that correlates to the desire, the thing that you seek to have in your life. If there is no current Karma blockage, then you should be able to attain that which is desired rather simply, if not always quickly. What you seek comes to you very simply. It almost seems to glide into your hands as you request. You stand back and marvel at that receipt!

But, if there is Karma that is blocking you, built up fear or thoughts of trepidation surrounding the request will come to mind and surround the request again. These will force the desire to cool, instead of heating up. Heat-is the contributing factor in attainment. The passion for the receipt of the object or circumstance that is requested heats up the process of manifestation and draws the thing to you.

However, fears stop the process and shut the wish desire down, *halting* the action. FEAR is the number one reason people do not receive what they ask for. Fear, NOT Karma, not preciously held beliefs, nor previous lost lives of dementia, creating new chaos in current lifetimes. No, it is fear. Unresolved fear from past lives, for which there are usually many fears accumulated and carried over, unresolved, into future lifetimes.

How then, does the individual overcome these accumulated fears? In any lifetime, this is the ultimate challenge that humans must learn, to *overcome their fears by simply living, stepping up to the fear directly, looking at it nakedly and passing through it.* This takes time and practice.

Pushing through fear, time and time again as it resurfaces, creates a new format, of which certainty is then replacing fear, while confidence is replacing confusion. The aspirant who addresses his issues is putting the pace on in resolving his fear-based thoughts and grows to assume greater success in his life.

This allows the person, after many successive tries at it, to grow stronger out of the process of applying these metaphysical techniques. Eventually, the aspirant will be able to make leaps of faith and connect with the down pouring of good blessings which are flowing constantly from the other side to Earth, constantly accessible upon acknowledgement; drawing down grace to the soul through prayer and daily meditation.

Love can conquer us all if we would let it and will it so! However, even love, *receipt of a destined love mate, can be halted with fear!* Have you ever had a love mate stare you in the face and suddenly you never hear from him or her again? You thought *"that face"* would reappear in your life and you could build a dream with him or her but it never materializes? You never know exactly what happened, it just causes both parties to move on and go their separate ways. To wit we say, *"Fear causes an interruption of all services"*.

Even the promised receipt of a destined lover can be stopped, the actual delivery of that lover to your door is stopped *IF YOUR FEAR IS GREAT ENOUGH TO PUT CAUSE IN IT.*

Love is not the solution all would have it be. There is no love to vanquish all the ills of the planet. The human condition is frail until the aspirant learns to study and meditate, growing up through many rounds of evolution. We see this process holds the very promise of the universe; that all humankind can *ascend* is the main focus. I would ask you to consider the following premise:

The Earth is an ongoing cosmos and all things within its scope of reality are in motion. Nothing is without growth. Nothing is without change, form, and dimension and the size of all things is in swift variation.

We can explain thus: that all things are moving forward, although it may not appear so, it is so. Nothing stands still forever. So, it takes great patience for us to assist humanity through these long, cold and many times unproductive periods.

Eons we wait for humankind to come of age. This planet is now of age. It is ready for the turning point and the biggest growth period for humanity on Planet Earth is here, starting right here in this time frame.

As we go forward, humanity has the opportunity to awaken from its dead-like state of thought to find itself with a lively presentation of choices straight ahead of itself. This is an amazing future as humanity grows to the spiritual side. We see it happening as we speak.

America is now leaning and looking intently for purpose, as it sorely needs purpose in viewing the state of the universe. In consideration of that fact, the United States is in the vanguard of civilization. The world will look to the United States for the leadership role. The United States of America is the flagship of the planet. All rest with her ability to lead civilization forward.

We say the best and the brightest will lead as they have before and rest assured, it is no mistake that they are living at this time, as this is a pivotal point, where the world needs to move forward and springboard into the spiritual side of development. It is essential that we pick up the pace for civilization through the understanding of the fact that *we are all one*.

That oneness is the core belief that will carry humanity forward and we will assist in this forward motion. We are the great teachers that stand ready to assist. Humanity has but to follow what it will be inclined to do as we go forward. By this we mean, as the urge toward the higher engagement of the spiritual side occurs for humanity, the physical world will change for the better, as all will learn to be more than what they are today. All will grow and the manifestation of what they produce upon the Earth will be more useful for the total overall environment. Civilization will reap the benefit and the reward. The children that come through will then be the beneficiaries of all these marvelous changes that will come into fruition.

Inventions that will be coming forward will come to Earth, as the people of Earth master control of themselves and not use things for the purposes of self-destructiveness.

Nationalisms that are causing disruption of populations of the Earth, one at the throat of the other, due to engagement of war for power upon the Earth, will cease.

Wars are in the natural order of things until societies develop upon all levels on the planet. Societies will come about and not stand for the future to contain war; they will learn the methods and ways of curtailing war and the *prelude to war*.

Now, upon the Earth is the quickened pace, due to NUCLEAR POWER! You see that this is expanding and this is a great potentiality of destructiveness. Yet, we worry about this and hope that we will be able to adequately lift the spiritual side of humanity before the destructiveness grows out of control. That is the real reason for books such as this and the real reason for the information to come to humanity swiftly as the time is limited and we need to see that humanity turns this corner swiftly. It is of the greatest importance that the spiritual side of humanity be emphasized.

As spirituality is emphasized, the focus and very desires of what humanity wants for itself will change for the better. All things will change to the upside and the planet and all peoples on the planet will live with better conditions.

Imprisonment, slavery of others, or other deplorable human conditions will no longer be tolerated upon the Earth, as they will no longer be viewed as necessary, or acceptable. Humanity will outgrow its crude levels of existence developing from ignorance and fear of lack.

What was once an assortment of evils will diminish as the overall soul groups and soul level of the planet gets a much-needed lift up! Much needed consequences for all then, the good consequences of right actions will bring about amazing changes for humanity. To wit, civilization will be so far removed from the anguishing conditions that exist in so many parts of the world today, that this new world that will come about will not even resemble its former state. *SO MOTE IT BE.*

CHAPTER TWO

CASTING AND PROJECTION OF A MATE

TO BEGIN WITH, selection of a mate is a delicate thing. How do we draw our mates? Did you ever wonder about this mating process? If you would give me your full attention; I would like to add here a fuller understanding of this process from our prospective, from this side, the side of Spirit, which is to assist humanity in this process to assure that couples succeed in coming together, especially those with leadership potential, that will lift up humanity.

The process begins first from this side. After each lifetime the Soul comes here for a resting period, then a period of educational pursuit wherein the Soul picks up with intense learning, leaving right off from where it was in the previous Earth lifespan.

Oftentimes the Soul needs quite a bit of help from us to fully analyze what it actually did with its opportunity in the previous lifetime that preceded the Spirit life return here. Once our guides assist with that process, it is determined what the Soul chooses to do in the next lifetime. We assist this process here, but we do not fully decide the choice for the individual Soul as the actual lifetime opportunities and circumstances can proceed differently once enactment begins and rebirth takes place. A general outline, however, always exists for the Soul, implanted in the heart seed atom before the Soul takes up additional rebirth.

The Higher-Self is the guide and will offer help subconsciously through the many facets of expressed reality as the progression of the life is in force. The Higher-Self fosters, through always loving and overshadowing, an exchange of actions which co-sponsor the basic terms of the outline established on this side for the Soul. This outline was determined by the Soul in conjunction with a governing body of spiritual guides, assisting prior to the succeeding rebirth. That loving assistance, in these matters, is given before the Soul is released to begin its journey back into physicality on the Earth plane. In this way, the precious time on Earth will be well spent. At least, that is the positive thought stream we send over with the Soul into its next lifespan. We inspire them *to begin with great love and high hopes from* here, as they go out.

The combination of *three things* then, comes into play upon reaching Earth and starting a new lifetime. There is the matter of *Karma* from all previous lives. There is the matter of *accord* with the next family that the Soul chooses to come through for the next life of human expression and experience and then there is the *emphasis on the learning*, which the Soul wishes to accomplish in the next lifetime. The details of these choices are quite specific and marvelous, as we work hard here to involve ourselves in the spiritual guiding for the success of the next mission on Earth.

This is always our mission, "success", never failure. We do not threaten or create fear in these choices. Never is that so. We wish to say firmly that we do not engage in revenge or retribution for prior events. This is many times misunderstood when the subject of Karma comes up. We will expand upon the existing knowledge in these matters as we move along into future chapters.

Akashic records, Soul records, are retained from lifetime to lifetime. Each Soul has its own recorded history. Brain center strong points, which have been based on previous lifetime emphasis will be considered and reviewed. Midpoints, wherein secondary career and gift development choices that the Soul has worked up to and had previous involvement with, are also reviewed beforehand and considered in the overview, prior to re- entry.

Then there is the matter of what the Soul longs to achieve going forward. All of these things come into play and form a basis for attraction; attraction to the next lifetime and a need to re-enter the physical world to have the experiences desired and necessary to reduce Karma and proceed upward through the necessary spiritual evolution in rounds.

As the Soul matures with its determination on this side, the heart seed atoms and other atoms start to warm up, becoming activated just before the Soul is ready to take up another lifespan. Then, when the Soul is ready for the next Earth journey, we help them find the family, the mating pair that is ready for the receipt of their reconstituted essence. Then, the Soul nears the couple through the astral projection process and the Soul seeking to be reborn is *literally attracted into the world of matter*, physically again; as the mating pair has sexual intercourse, the Soul is drawn into the couple via frequency vibration and physical attraction laws, which govern this matter. This is basically how the process works.

The sex of the child is chosen by the Soul before entry and is based on what is required by the Soul to complete its planned activities in the next lifetime. Karma plays a part too. Usually, the subject of male or female is a distinctive one and these choices and characteristics behind these choices will be discussed at a future point in this book.

For now, we wish to speak further on the mating pair; it is no mistake "whom" we mate with. This is a planned coming together. What people do not know on this pairing is truly remarkable as we see it.

Humanity is having a hard time with its spirituality. *Imagine the problem* in trying to put forward these metaphysical concepts without prior training and education? We say basic education in cosmos evolution and developments would be the way to receive the best appreciation of context and application of principles, as a solid foundation would be established through many years of study.

We wish to say that our guides will help all that study cosmic teachings. As the aspirant studies, we encourage their efforts subconsciously, as they go about their daily lives.

Grasping these possibilities, expressed in the teachings, is **a** difficult thing for most of humanity which is not ready, nor has it given itself over to the zeal vital for the spiritual upheaval which is usually required in order to create the desire necessary for acquiring these higher wisdom studies and knowledge.

To wit, it is to be explained further. But for today, let us begin with the process of attracting our mates. Groups from our side work with groups from your side. Individuals are literally, "set-up" to meet each other. This is not by chance. We simply have senders and receivers; of which you are now becoming aware.

By groups on your side, we speak of other forms of spiritual entities, angels, guardians, spiritual brothers assigned to specific groups to guide, lead and inspire proper direction for humanity's growth, just as right now Madame, we are working openly with you and you, with distinction, are consciously being guided to your next mate. We are trying to also bring him to the knowledge and desire of you from the astral plane of intervention.

Materialization of the mate takes time and depends completely on how well this "leading" process goes. Some individuals are easily led. Some are extremely difficult due to their stubbornness and reticence. To wit, we say, "patience is an absolute requirement for us on this side."

Now, as to the exactitude of this mating process, the paths cross for the two individuals at the point that the groundwork has been accomplished from our end.

The suitor, the male, must be ready for the receipt of the female and he must be a good match up. His appetite for her is governed by previous attempts to find her. As he eliminates preceding women from his path, no longer being drawn to them, he moves closer to the real target. This is done through matching correspondence. He narrows his own field to find his mate, picking her out via the sense of matching correspondences. As she also will be going through the same process with other male candidates, so also is she eliminating prospective mates and proceeding to hone in on the correct target, the correct signal to be picked out of the chaos, her mate.

This entire process is most beautiful and completely subconscious for most humans, as we have been preparing humanity for proper assignment of mates this way for eons and it works quite well.

Then, when the two finally meet, the initial chemistry comes into motion and the field becomes "lit up" filled with excitement and enthusiastic feelings upon the initial interaction of the couple. In finding each other they have found the "treasure", the greatest moment of their lives. There is no greater blessing than finding one's true love to join in our Earth journey! We would encourage all people to understand that the initial "sparking" between two people is the catalyst for change and that that moment is significant and never to be walked from, shied away from, or feared.

With purpose and trust we must love our mates and then our destinies can reveal to us so very much more; but, if we choose to *ignore* this initial sparking, this initial meeting, *if it is glossed over,* then the mate may move out of range for a relationship and the timing and necessary "heat and excitement" is lost, maybe lost for this lifetime… completely.

We wish to stress then, that all those who look for and dream today of finding their exact mate *follow their hearts completely. All other things in life are secondary gifts compared with this, this* one, this special cornerstone, *the "love mate".* Wrap a world around that foundation and you are to find the greatest experience of loving. The design is flawless when the two find each other. The basic design and ingredients are flawless. The joy is in the building of your dreams together.

But, until found and acknowledged, experiencing the love mate, is not understood. This great sharing can be and building in unison is wonderful, we say. From here, as we remember life in the human form, we say, it is the very best, this thing called *Love!* We wish to encourage all to love and to find their love mates; experiencing in abundance; life, liberty, and the pursuit of happiness.

And so on that high note, we end here this chapter as a basic understanding of how these things come about… we will talk further about love mates throughout many of our chapters in this book, an important discourse into the humanities; human consciousness gaining through ascendance of knowledge and intelligence throughout the ages.

CHAPTER THREE

Equality, A State of Mind and Action For The Universe

IT HAS OFTEN BEEN SAID that mankind has no roots. This is not so. The roots of mankind are from the beginning of creation. All are created equally under the plan of the Godhead. All begin with the same process and come forward for the same purpose.

As these Souls come into being, the experience of living on Planet Earth creates its tarnish on each individualized Soul, lifetime after lifetime. This is the weight of the matter of accumulated Karmic debt, which has to be resolved and balanced out with fresh offsets of right action. This is what draws the Soul back into the physical world time and time again. This is the need to rectify itself.

Pursuant to this, all Souls return to learn and grow brighter in the Spirit with each re-entry into the Earth plane, the plane of matter. It may seem foreign, *uneven and unequal*, but the knowledge of previous lives is not easily or readily available to the Soul while it is living its current incarnation.

Although the Higher-Self contains the filing system, the history of the Soul's experiences throughout all of its human life waves, Akashic Records, these histories are not easily opened and revealed. Very few human beings accept the existence of these records, let alone understand that this part of the human mind can be communicated with directly. We repeat this truth. That it can be communicated with directly for guidance and spiritual help. We will speak more about this property of the functioning, operational brain system later. It is a complicated field of discourse for a separate chapter.

If there seems to be a preferential set of rules and circumstances for one race of humankind and a set of differential rules and conditions for another group, which seems fraught with partiality towards determent, this is only an illusion of thought, as the Soul determines its own destiny and which group it will participate in, principally. This is not by chance. This is part of the overall planned encounter from the other side, which the Soul will try to follow, intuitively, as it goes.

The nationalism of where the Soul takes up housing in any one lifetime is something that is picked out ahead of re- entry. When the selection of the family for the Soul to come to is finalized on this end, the national aspect is taken into consideration.

As part of the Soul's overall decision, the consideration of what the Soul wants to achieve and what it has to work off in that lifetime, in the way of Karma, is also considered. We have touched on this consideration in the previous chapter. We have spoken of the family connection, also, in the previous chapter. We have talked about the process for the overview and how the Soul chooses what it will do from the perspective of choice, from this side, with our council members, before the Soul kicks off from here to take up life in the body again.

Once more, we return to the inevitable subject of mindset, and the choice of viewpoints; inequality vs. equality, equanimity or chaotic unevenness? There is much to know about this subject. Especially, considering that as a whole, Planet Earth is at a turning point, coming out of the dark ages of perceived lack, into the technological age of rapid advancement, on all fronts. Planet Earth, *with proper application and discernment, is at the helm of creative thinking.*

Much of the world's population sees the world with total limitation and sees themselves as *almost powerless* within the larger scope of things. It seems so out of kilter if one only looks at it from the perspective view of so many humans. So many humans then, with blinders on and a lack of prevailing wisdom, seeing themselves as not being "participants", but as victims. While all that is newly creating within the world's force is at the mercy of the developing mindset of the people, which often leans to a negative bent, *learning to lean towards the positives is essential!*

The opportunities wait for humanity to take advantage, to catch the winds of change, make the required efforts *of positive actions, and step into the forward motion of materialized results; results that were put forward with heated desire.* To bring forward what they require to meet their own needs and establish a peaceful setting, an orderly existence, for themselves and others within society requires structure, discipline, and patient leadership. This leadership must be determined to advance and be tenacious enough to succeed, beyond any repeated attempts that have temporarily failed to produce the desired results.

Eons of time, humanity has struggled to come out of the chaos, out of the dark ages of civilization. Now, at this time, freedom is best expressed as equality for all, rights protected justly, through laws that promise in a constitutional sense, rights under the law.

Humanity is blessed with at least getting that far in the most *democratized* nations on the Planet Earth that are in existence today. But conditions exist in other nations today, nations that are not free, where this is not the case, and the rule of law and respect and protection for individual rights under the law does not exist!

Consider the state of other peoples that exists in countries under the rule of tyrants? Consider the consequences of subjected peoples under the terrible, deplorable conditions of slavery? I could go on and on with the ills that still exist all over the Planet Earth and are *allowed to exist*.

These conditions exist as the governing bodies of the world view borders, respect borders, keep agreements to remain in denial, unless they are "personally" interested due to selective predetermination of the need to protect necessary natural resources, at certain points of world geography, for their respective countries. Or, to defend themselves against the tyrants and protect their homelands that could be threatened in the future, with tyrants left undeterred and to their own devices.

Now, equality, when you consider all of that, for the people enslaved is a different matter, isn't it? And what is the responsibility of the rest of the world to respond to those held in slavery, the ones still held in bondage? Much lip service is given to their plight, but not enough emphasis worldwide, by the top seven nations that could make a difference; lack of attention to these things, gives one pause from this side.

We say that the time will come when the spiritual state of the planet will require everyone to be equal, everyone to share in the blessing and providence of freedom, in full recognition that it is a natural, higher order of component values, this thing that is eternal spiritually, within the hearts and minds of all humanity!

At such a time the pace of things will have calmed down, believe it or not. The continued fear of humanity towards "lack" and the concerns of lack create and assure the continued state of lack. If it could be understood that there is no lack, that it is the perspective of the human mind that chooses to view it in that manner, all things would change and rightly so, as there is no lack. There is only abundance. However, how can one get to abundance while perceiving there is only lack? *Right thinking, right action!*

The state of the world is constituted upon the state of mind of humanity. Collective intelligence exists! This is not a fantasy. This is real. A real bank of collective intelligence exists! And humanity is adding and subtracting to it daily via thought and deed.

If that could be understood, more Souls would pay attention to what it is they do, what it is they give their daily energies to, in thought and deed! Look to those things to make or break humanity in the future then.

How do we change things for the better? How does humanity overcome its natural tendency to think along the lines of valuing itself as unequal? Humanity needs to look at this from the opposite position of a static equation. It is not static and never was. This universe is a moving force. It is a beautiful vehicle for change and we that live it, whether your side or ours, have the privilege of invention and convention of thought. We have the privilege of educating ourselves to the higher responding factors of this universe. It is the responsibility then, to the best and the brightest on the Planet Earth, to see that the "inventions" and "conventions" of thought that govern the necessary changes come into fruition and serve to profit the lesser groups, as well as the predominant masses.

It is up to these preeminent groups from all of the nations upon the planet to be the "vanguard" of the future. To these Souls is the directive to aspire to lead humanity through the necessary changes, which will assure the successful feeding and caring of the populace of the planet going forward. The point being, that the everyday needs of humanity at large can be reduced and that human concerns can be lifted to a more spiritual level of existence. New science will be key!

Inventions are developed, conceptually, on the astral plane, by large groups of scientists. They work to further these inventions in the spirit of unity. There is no concern of authorship. All products and inventions are developed in the true spirit of equality. All work together in the spirit of brotherhood and love of humanity and the opportunity to serve is the motivating factor.

Proper use of what is created is very important, as important as the invention itself. However, to bring in new inventions, *before* the use of the products is understood and determined to be for the general purpose of usefulness for humanity, is to bring something forward ahead of its time.

We are careful as to the timing, as it is most important not to risk entering too soon to the Earth plane *with the thoughts that will produce the invention*, as we want to be absolutely sure, that the proper use of the thing that comes will be for the benefit of the planet and not be misused and hurt the progress of humanity. Where a significant invention could be construed for detrimental purposes by the unscrupulous, better to hold conveyance of the creation over here, and suspend entry until a later date in time, when conditions have improved.

We see then, to the proper timing of the receipt of the idea on your side and the development is guided also. Receipt of the invention and authorship, patents, are essential on the Earth, but here, Spirit-side, we know the truth behind the invention. Before it ever gets to your side, the world of physicality, it fully exists here.

It is in this way that inventions proceed from here to there. Of course, we do not claim that this truth will be greatly appreciated or accepted by the Earth's scientific groups, because it is usually arrogance that will prevail with them when it comes to claims of product ownership and initial creation.

This method of how inventions and ideas come to development would most likely be considered inconceivable on the part of the Earth plane science groups, as these groups tend to be hard to lead into a metaphysical bent or *an openness* towards a path of discovery that is not seemingly tangible. Immediate credibility is "all" to so many there on Earth and incredible leaps of faith are hard to come by.

CHAPTER FOUR

NATIONS AT WAR, PEACE AT HAND

TO BEGIN WITH, in this 21st century the subject of war and peace is as fraught with pain as in any other period of civilization. We, the guardians, had hoped that humanity would be a whole lot more spiritually driven at this point. This would make it easier to produce harmony all over the planet. Now we must accept that from this vantage point- No! It is not harmony; it is not all sunlight and prose.

So, what are the dilemmas that are holding up humanity from obtaining world peace for the Planet Earth?

These are some of the most perilous times we have ***ever experienced*** with Planet Earth in tow and at the balance. Today, with the growing opportunities for more nations to obtain the ability to become nuclear powers, the times are becoming downright dangerous.

Humanity, in the Western world cultures, is all caught up with its daily chores of earning a living. In the United States, for example, what we see happening is that the larger decisions are left to your congress, senate and presidency to encompass the globe with good judgment and fairness in what they do and what they attempt to do.

Therefore, people in the United States of America are, literally, at the mercy of their representatives, whom they have voted into office. Too often these representatives choose the path of least resistance, wherever it appears, as we see from here.

We say justice and liberty often go by the wayside when the easy path is chosen instead of the right path requiring harder action, harder choices and more commitment to the larger picture, the global overview of Planet Earth.

Short-term solutions to problems cause short-term relief. Larger commitments to changes require larger commitments of mind, body and soul. Core actions or inactions on the part of representatives speak louder than their words. The "need to play it safe" is often a pullback position for most people, as so few want to hang out on a limb on any issue good, bad, or indifferent.

Herd mentality, even at the highest level of political life, is a real thing. Oftentimes this is a deterrent, all by itself, which causes stagnation of progress. Personal fears will cause many to sideline issues that could have been achieved successfully, if there was simply a stronger leader, with heart and perseverance, determined to work harder and forego the obvious easy road of staying within the boundaries of the herd mentality.

Whether one chooses to defer or take action when required, there are no easy answers for world peace.

In the previous chapters we talked about equality. We talked about the larger, wealthier, and more successful western nations of the world having a responsibility for bringing along the lesser developing nations. We said that it was up to them to lead. We said it was imperative that they do so, with the world consciousness being lifted up to a more spiritual level, resulting from these leading countries themselves becoming more peaceful and harmonic, the consequences of their own good, solid, and right actions.

This comes as a result of firm, right choices, to invest time, resources, and efforts properly. Timely efforts are being made all over the planet to keep the container lid on nuclear power. Yet, the world has gone from G-7 to G-8 nations and beyond, scrambling now to stop the neighboring, smaller countries of the Middle East from killing each other were they to obtain nuclear power, which is a real concern, even as we write here today.

And this is no easy task for these nations: Jerusalem has always been a point of interest and a hotbed of conflicts, almost from the beginning of time! That the Arabs and Jews still have not found a way to co-exist does not surprise us, as the religious differences are still a point of dissention and will cause an ongoing basis for non-agreements of treaties and preliminary alliances.

Territorial claims have also held this area of the world in great conflict of interest, one group against the other; history is replete with centuries of ruthless, bloody battling upon the land, people dying at issue, human lives given up too easily to warfare in the day's balance of trade of gunshots from one to the other. Violence is for so many still the only solution, still the weapon of choice.

The Middle East remains the focus of war as we write. It was the hope of your then current President, Mr. Bush, to save the world with his intervention against the tyrants of the Middle East. History will record how he struggled to do so, at great cost of lives of countrymen and lives of allies. The national budget of your country and the allied countries has also been greatly affected.

Still, the need to **stay the course** is a real need, as liberty cannot prevail and proceed in that area of the world without the strong arm of the United States of America and allied nations that would see freedom and democracy come to the Middle East and eventually, the entire planet.

Then, there are the considerations of China and Korea. We wish to say here, that we will do all that we can to foster and support cooperation with all nations, at all levels of power all over the Earth. We will, as guardians, try to instill a fierce acceptance and leaning towards tolerance, nation to nation. Within all open channels of communication and to all peoples, of all countries, do we send the vibrations to the Planet Earth that will increase the desire, within the hearts of men, towards the spirit of tolerance of each other's belief system and full acceptance of each other's right to exist.

Diplomacy, across the board at all meetings of super powers, or lesser groups, would be the tenor and demeanor, wherein we would look to inspire with our thoughts into these minds that meet and convene at the power centers all over the planet. We will do all that we can and we would hope that we could work quickly now to lead the minds of the people of Earth to a spiritual bent, which will give this planet a much-needed lift up.

It is time to come to the realization that beyond what Earth has produced so far lies the materialization of future needs being met easier as mankind learns to stand tall for each other, brother to brother in the freewheeling global marketplace of which all are open to the possibility of profit and all are ready to bid on a basis of equal standing without aggression, large and small nations at peace, side by side.

Spirituality, a rise to same, is the answer here. The Earth has built itself up now, to the age of technological knowledge and operation. The technological advances that will come through now will aid humanity to obtain and meet its daily needs for food and shelter.

These times are coming swiftly now, quicker than in the past because of the ability to mass-produce and to integrate and mass-produce from the already established levels of scientific understanding. It is not as if we are at the beginning. We are, in fact, at a midway point, where we say the technological achievements of the near future will open the doors to a greater good, the type that will be revolutionary as compared to today.

Today, it is a driven society base in the Western civilizations. All are busy producing what it is they require, sustaining their chosen ways of life. Americans for instance, keep a quickened steady pace, many we say, too busy, being already committed to large obligations, so there is very little time given to the matter of "thinking beyond the gap". The gap being, the larger issues of the planet and the necessary changes required to move this great planet forward with charity, love, and provisions for everyone.

Today there is "no knowledge of us" for most. Metaphysical concepts and cosmos considerations are often filed under material, aberrant considerations, for the lunatic fringe. Those that would like to speak with us, don't! Because to begin with, they don't even know that we exist. This planet is young to the universal understandings that are, in fact, derived from the dynamics of prior advances made beyond this planet's current stage of progressive evolution of species and humankind. We are the logos that precede any beginning of any planet that is to be inhabited

Believe in us, the planetary guardianship groups from the Spirit-side, of which there are many, *Astara* being just one leading group of the many. Our pledge is to guide and protect all through the many rounds of evolutionary development, from dense matter into highly intelligent, sentient beings.

We are the unseen forces that govern through love and devotion to humanity over the course of weightless eons into a rarified human perception.

It is difficult, if not nearly impossible, to penetrate the blocked off mindset of the scientific communities. They are often hard-nosed groups. They are often self-centered and arrogant. Pride often puts them at a great disadvantage to themselves and their goals. Their goals are not often lofty with idealism, but we say, lofty with intent to increasing personal wealth and power while pumping up the bottom line of their corporation's balance sheets.

Often the advantages of considerations beyond those horizons of greed are not even acknowledged at the highest corporate level. The view is often a static view, a piecemeal parceling along the lines of intentions to "look" like they are sponsoring good community activity and good charity for those that work within the company. But, lip service and action with honest intent to follow through for the common good are, too often in the end, found in juxtaposition, contradicting each other and many times canceling out any benefits to be derived.

Many levels of procrastination exist upon the Earth today and there is not enough concentrated effort to move this world towards the larger peace, the larger harmony. Mankind proceeds slowly as if within a mood of stubbornness - *irritable children needing a nap.*

And then there is playtime! Entertainment seems to be a shifting tied to emotion. People of the Western cultures are looking to escape their small realities every day, in many different ways.

Upon many faces we see discontent. There is the feeling on Planet Earth that nothing will satisfy. Nothing but greed, nothing but money seems to be the mindset that we observe.

Nothing but money will solve the problems of the planet is the thought of the populace, globally. But, when money is obtained, humanity seems to simply want more and even then, they cannot answer, what is enough?

Again, the determination as to what really is at work within the hearts and minds of humanity comes into question. This is a time for self-examination. Healing our *nations* and our*selves* begins with the assessment of our wounds and how they came about. Emotional balancing or the lack thereof creates its own counterbalance. This is an ongoing process, back and forth.

Nations will continue to be at war until humanity grows to the realization that war itself is too costly, racking up a severe tally in both human and economic terms. Stepped up warring, wherein eminent destruction to the core of civilization becomes possible, is a risk that humanity should never take again. ***The days of Atlantis come to mind. We do not want to repeat that ending.***

CHAPTER FIVE

CHALLENGES FOR A CIVILIZED WORLD

TO BEGIN WITH, this world is not totally civilized, is it? We have many parts of the world that are a throwback in time with their actual points of geography being almost unmapped. I am thinking of many of the tribes that exist as we speak, unknown. Many of them exist deep within the Indian cultures off of the coast of the Amazon region. Yet, they exist, within their belief system, and have every right to co-exist with the upscale British travelers that come to observe them on safari, or to catch a glimpse of their uncivilized world from the edges of their riverboats, as they are passing by.

So, we see how this is different, don't we? Some of humanity being highly developed and going ahead in their lives within the technological societies of which they live in, while others are completely existing within a world that is tribal, driven by ancient warrior belief and remote barrenness.

Therefore, mankind has his work cut out for him, as *all* must come about and look up to the attainment of the spiritual evolution that is calling them to progress every day.

Every day, the vibrations from the higher worlds travel to the Earth. It is a sort of spiritual flow from the higher planes to these planes of Earth. Yet it falls upon humanity and some pick up the nourishment in thought that is sent, while others are taking longer to get a feeling for the movement that is already in motion, waiting to be accessed.

We have stated in previous chapters that the ones on the planet with the most going for them, have the responsibility to lead the others to see that the planet makes the necessary steady progress towards achieving balance of all things, balancing of all peoples, one to the other. We have said too, that this is no easy course for humankind and that we, the guardians, will do our best to assist.

It comes as no surprise to us, the guardians, to see the planet and the people of Earth struggling so, as we turn this page of progress. This is to be expected, as much of this world revolves around national thought, individual thought, group thought, community thought, and on and on it goes with much of that thought being contrary to the other.

Here in the USA many religious thoughts prevail, one alongside the other because the rule of law exists and because this nation is one that accepts, *with tolerance*, many religious originations and churches, side by side, with no problem. This is an intelligent level that is not shared all over the Planet Earth, however!

So the first big challenge for humanity and perhaps the hardest one for the entire universe is **TOLERANCE, the ability to co- exist! You are blessed to have this existing and prevailing in the great United States of America.** Also, this wisdom exists in other Western civilized nations that are as solid on this understanding as you are there in the USA. *The universal brotherhood of all peoples* is a noble and honestly achievable thing to bring about, as more nations on the Earth find acceptance of this principle and put that forth as a concept, which is the cornerstone of their constitutions in principles and rights.

How do we help spread this noble concept of *tolerance*?

Right action and self-example! Those that have it, must live it and by doing so spread this beautiful blessing upon the Earth. Those that have it must spread it across the airwaves in speech. Express it in our books of literature, our staged dramas in our theaters and of course, present it in our motion picture films. Showing that worlds wherein love and tolerance exist will show that happiness abounds with these principles at the core.

Speak it openly! ***TOLERANCE!*** Step up and speak with tolerance in the choice of your words, your humanity, and the words that precede your deeds. In your actions bear witness to your words. Bear witness through tolerance in your actions, being selective in what you choose to participate in. In your business and office relationships, those that have tolerance stand up for those that would be infringed upon with intolerance, taking the offenders gently to the side and expressing your unhappiness with their intolerant remarks or poor actions that have hurt another without justice, without cause. These would be very basic methods to live by on a daily basis and would improve society and better mankind with purity of heart, which flourishes upon the Earth, producing a doubling and tripling of blessings that ripples through the waters of time and causes.

Injustice, we say, is the next most challenging thing, as tyranny still exists on Planet Earth. Slavery of humankind still exists. Torture and political imprisonment at will, still exist. Genocide and ruthless murdering of millions still exist! Warring and terrorism are daily events in too much of this world, taking its toll at a high price in human wastelands and human suffering.

As the armies of elemental brutality and imposing force behave in unscrupulous and often scurrilous ways, the nations that are free rise up firmly, protecting their borders, protecting their homelands, protecting their peoples against rebel invasions and invaders that would seek to challenge established freedom and democracy domains.

It is hard to imagine a world more at each other's throat than the one that you are living in today. There is no escaping this reality, as the evening news broadcasts carried by satellite communication systems all over the planet is replete with the daily blood fest, the daily pillaging, the daily suffering that is making humanity ill and keeping it in spiritual chains.

Humanity must grow beyond this stage of killing each other for survival, inconsistence with a core need to rise to a higher spiritual truth; the truth that we must all live together in harmony; the truth that we are all brothers and sisters in freedom. *That freedom* is the natural order and birthright of all of humanity, no matter what country or domain of authority one is born into. *This then is the larger stage upon which humanity must seek to dwell.*

Getting there is possible with great intent and purposeful action on the part of the people of Planet Earth. Wisdom must prevail, a greater wisdom that will come only through an accord with the higher principles of love and trust, one to the other, which will lift this planet higher. With that promise and purpose comes the understanding and concurrent knowledge to implementation, which will flow naturally into the minds and lives of all humanity.

Many will be given the vanguard position to lead all to this new homeland security ... each other! Those that are the wisest need to lead and not follow the tyrants, responding with equal retorts of violence maiming this planet further, pushing it further along the lines of destructiveness that can only serve to underscore future violence.

What then, is the proper course of action against the reigning rule of existing tyrants and tyrant-like nations of brutality upon the Earth? The bullet will not serve well here, only short term. Only winning them over will serve humankind long term. By that I mean, introducing them into a better way of life. Taking them into our world, a world that would be civilized in all matters, on a daily basis of operation. How can this be achieved now? Easily? No, but ending warring of all sort would be a great start!

Of course, you would ask me, Rama, how is this possible today? First it begins *with believing that it is possible.* You cannot start up that road without the belief that there is a road to start on. Believing gets us into motion.

Planning effectively, in critical stages, will take the greatest minds on the planet, all working together to achieve this worldwide goal. With such a goal at heart, war machines and future costs to house and maintain such weaponry could be staved off and eventually stopped. We could turn the world's resources to the primary business of creating a better world.

Landmasses could be freed of poisonous material now being buried and threatening the environment. Nuclear weapons could be pulled out of service and retired to warehouses and eventually never need be put into the position for redeployment, as humanity would have outgrown its belief in the old system of warfare as a measure for settling anything of consequence on the Planet Earth.

Humanity would not be in peril. It would be in the pursuit of true brotherhood and a brighter tomorrow could come.

Creature comforts could remain, but with changes that would accommodate proper considerations to the environment wherein they are placed.

Weapons retired and daily work for pay would be for the pursuit of a world no longer in chains to old negative thought patterns, which beg repeating needlessly, lifetime after lifetime, century in and out!

People would rule, not their world circumstances; *Mind, body and Soul richly engaged in these positive endeavors* would live in harmony on the planet, forming international alliances for a specific achievement that would serve the needs of humanity, much the way it does exist in the spirit world life, where authorship becomes a moot point, but the advancement of humanity through scientific discovery is *all.*

So wonderful would be the richness then on this planet, that it would find its abundance, its fullness coming faster and would come in naturally, as the day follows night now, as all of humanity would know the truth; That we live on, that we are more than our bodies, that we are more than we appear to be. Most of all, that we are here, each and every *Soul with purpose* and that *we are God's greatest achievement!*

That each one of us has the potential to start and lead another planet in time, as this universe is full of additional planets that are barren now, but, at some future point in the sphere of universal rhythm and structure, these planets will come about and be destined to provide the necessary elementals to house and provide life forms of human type. Human type then, will come to such planets.

We are the beginning. We are the elementals. We are the origins and we are here on this planet Earth watching and tenderly gauging its progress. We will guide, but know that humans here must rise now and *spearhead their futures, if they choose, with wisdom.* If they chose to listen to this book of wisdom being dictated, they will know that so great is the future that it cannot be understated here, the gravity of the world is huge.

This world is necessary to begin worlds elsewhere in the universe. These things are complex understandings from the beginning of time and given with clear instructions from the Godhead, which is providential for all of us, now through all of eternity, *so mote it be.*

Astara -Highlands Central, located above the Earth's atmosphere, is a leading guiding light force dedicated to the uplifting and education of humanity upon Planet Earth. We congratulate all seekers upon this planet. All are welcome to study, to learn and to grow with the experiences of spirituality thinking and emphasis into their daily life practice.

This is the way of the biblical disciples. This is the way of tutorials into mastership of self, wherein there is no break of consciousness necessary, even at the point of leaving your physical body via death in the physical to rise here in the spirit. Although few of you will achieve that level of discipleship, adept to such capabilities at the time of transitioning to this side. One step at a time, one day at a time, is all that is required daily.

World greed and selfishness, which pervades Planet Earth from corner to corner, is the next most difficult challenge facing humanity. *If the true value of the Soul* were understood, then the value of the material world would take its proper place and humanity would not suffer to the great degree it has suffered throughout eons.

Astara-Highlands Central, located above the Planet Earth, is dedicated to the uplifting of the spirit, the body and the mind, which emphasis will teach the aspirant the true nature of his being; the true nature of his world, allowing him to put all other things in proper perspective. With that new information forming a baseline, it will change the face of the planet, one *Soul* seeker at a time being added to the mix of humankind.

All it takes is one soul, one spiritual leader, to change a large group of thought. One voice in the wilderness can lead a tribal group out of the darkness into the light. It is the belief system in the rational existence of mankind, beyond all other considerations, which has caused humanity so much trouble and continues to keep him tied to his Earthly chains, repeating lifetime after lifetime due to his retarding belief system that equates everything in terms of the material goods acquired.

This will change here on Earth, as more and more people attain material status and in conquering their worlds, realize that this achievement does not assure happiness and contentment. Only then will they look further and discover us, the mystery schools and we will lead them to further considerations through the inward process of deep study and proper application of the innate principles of the Spirit and how it actually operates.

Greed is the subject of so many on Earth that want so much. Selfishness is the order of the day in this world of many cultures. Generosity is seen with a limitation, all things being equal.

What good is achieved by hoarding goods and wealth for oneself when it cannot be taken one lifetime through to the next? Why not ask yourselves: What is the true meaning of success?

What is the true nature of the Spirit? What must I do to bring happiness to my immediate family and myself? Is there a better mode of life and living that would generate a more profound meaning to my life overall? These are but a few of the questions and the answers are many.

To begin with, greed brings with it many things that the Soul did not understand or perceive at the point of "wishing for wealth". Having more, one may find, means one must work obsessively harder to get more and then there is the matter of protecting the "more" that has been achieved. This is an uphill battle for a lifetime and does not assure that the physical body has adapted fully to the mental body, let alone the increase of spiritual enlightenment that one would hope to achieve after each lifetime - duration on Earth.

The subject of greed brings with it the subject of selfishness and the wants of the many, versus the wants and desires of the individual. Why do we want so much? Why are these cravings of humanity so everlasting, that we come into being again and again to obtain them? These goals create desires that burn on this side too and others would tell you in the spirit life, that there is no peace except found in rebirth to settle our accounts.

This is the purpose for rebirth. We come to Planet Earth taking on the flesh again and again to repeat and try to settle our accounts and improve. Each time we return to try and balance our new lives in better fashion than we did in the previous incarnations. These desires are ongoing from one span of time to the other.

It is not an easy thing to leave the heart behind. There is so much heart in rebirth, which brings us back to repeat our love with those Souls, whom we continue to have a need for, a hunger and desire for reunion again. This is not selfishness, but Karma in action.

Not all Karma is bad. Much of it is good. And what could be better than starting a new life, taking up where one left off, right alongside of a brother or sister, a dear one, who has shared deeply, happily, within our past lives?

There are many blessings on our roads that lie ahead of us. Many blessings indeed and no Souls are ever left to wander through these lifetimes alone. Never is one without one's guardian and appropriate helpers. So great is the need of humanity going forward that we consider it the highest order of things and are privileged to serve in the capacity that has been given to us to fulfill the plan, the overall plan of God, the Holy Creator of all worlds, all Universes. He is never without us and we are all in Him.

Selfishness and greed fall back from our minds when we begin to understand that the true rule of the planet is abundance. That there is no lack, except, as we perceive it in the human mind, which is groping at success so plaintively that it is blinded from the truth of the operation in the process. This will change as the principles of the operating system are understood and the overall belief system changes.

This is the time for humanity to come of age. The time is now and we see it coming from here. The hearts of humanity will grow brighter, as they believe more in love and brotherhood. All will change for the better, as the Planet Earth warms to a gentle spirit and general uplifting for all Souls. We are sending out these feelings, these vibratory changes, and waves of love vibrating to Planet Earth, as we speak upon these pages of this book.

Each and every moment there is the potential for the Soul to grow in wisdom of the knowledge that no Soul is without protection. All the Soul needs to do is believe it and pray for direction and one will receive that direction instantly.

To be able to see that one is getting the help may take some recognition patterns to be established *in the mind's eye*, the eye of the one perceiving a daily miracle as mere happenstance. Often, it is an angel that has answered a prayer and swiftly flies off. As simple as that; a miracle in receipt, yet, so swiftly received, that to the naked eye it was missed in translation…so much to learn! We will talk further in the ongoing chapters of this book.

CHAPTER SIX

WORLDS APART, WORLDS AFAR

AND IT WOULD SEEM to many there on Earth, that the "dead" are just that, "dead!" We are here to say that is not so. The dead are alive and well in the spirit on this side. There is life here, as we have said in earlier chapters. It is not the physical world of Earth however; still there are just as many things to do here as there. We do not just *"flit around" in the spirit*. There is a design here, in the spirit, for us. There exists a full guide plan on Earth, which all of you are following. Although you may not be aware that the plan is in force, it is standing behind all of your actions.

As we have said earlier, each soul leaves here with an overall blueprint of the new lifetime that he is to undertake before he leaves this side. No soul leaves here without that imprint going into the essence of the Oversoul, which is the monitoring system set in motion at the time that the new personage comes into rebirthing on the Planet Earth. So then, the Soul starts fresh.

However, the Higher-Self has the overview of all previous lifetimes and will manage itself with the understanding of all the information from its own resources that have been grouped together in adjoining information files, much like the operating system of the very device that you are using tonight, Madame, the computer. This is done here, in the spirit, without a hard copy. It is all software implementation on this side, so mote it be. The enlightenment that the soul then goes out with on the journey to Earth, we hope, will be uplifting and encouraging!

We cannot overrule the free will of humanity! However, we, the guardians and angelic light force bases from here, in the Spirit, *will do all we can to* encourage the soul so that it manages to perform in *a God-like manner* when choices are to be made. Once the choices are in, this is the rule for all of us here: to lead to the upside, to lead to the increasing of the spiritual light upon humanity, and to lift up the light base of Planet Earth.

This is the worlds apart and the worlds afar that describe the difference between your side and my side. It seems like these worlds are totally separate, but actually these worlds co-exist, like points of translucent film, each touching the other in a filamentary structure, each interrelating and yet functioning separately.

We have cogent knowledge of the two worlds interspersing from here, in the spirit. You on Earth, unless you are mediums, are not aware of the natural intersecting of our existences that happen as a natural occurrence, full time, every time, every minute, in all of the worlds.

Within God's universes, there is a law that governs beyond this law. One that is the larger law for everyone and *that is the law of co-realities.* By that I mean we are all bilingual in thought. We just don't know it, most of us, especially from your side; have no idea of the language spoken on our side. But those of us that are here, literally "hear" and we know that our language is as real as yours.

This language is designed to accommodate the needs of the essences of existence in the Spirit that are true for this side. In other words, there is no physical need for a body here, so the language that is required is something that works for us, which does not require vocal cords. Vocal cords are used on your side because you are all spirits encased in a human operating system with a human brain, and that is why we say that the flesh is an accommodating system of necessity.

In order to live on your side, on Earth, and fully participate in life, it is necessary to have a body. But here, we have the mind, we have the soul, we have the language, the solid art of communication, one to the other here, in the spirit, across all division of existence on our side. We do not need the body here, as this environment is of a higher density and could not evolve at the lower plane wherein humanity exists on Earth. The vibratory frequencies are designed in entirety to fit with the requirements, the level evolving. We engage, each eon, with what is required to move humanity through that process and proceed towards greater advancement through the experience of existence on Earth.

Now, this may sound to you a bit confusing, or at least complex. Yes, that's a true thing, complexity, but that is the way we know these things to be. These are necessary differences, stages of evolution, which we know to be so. For so long, we were there, as you are there on Earth and for so many here, Spirit-side, we see that many will take up life again in the human form. When it is time, they will contemplate completion of their studies here and for the progress of their soul, they will again, take up life in the Spirit, *within the human form.*

You might ask, how does a soul know when it is time to move on? Well, this is a difficult answer, but the spiritual teachers here, do their very finest work with the higher degrees of complexity, as we want to get it right for each soul. We want to be sure that they go back to Earth when the folks that they need are to be at the same places, as they will need to encounter them, so their very destinies will entwine with each other and that these necessary correlations will come about. This is why parents and relations are no mistake. Although, this may not be easily seen or understood on your side, there is a relationship to all that comes and goes.

Generally speaking, we would say that these relationships could have quite a beneficial effect on the accomplishments of the personalities that are returning to take up new lives on your side. By that I mean, most people do well with loves from the past and find greater happiness and fulfillment within these same family ties again and again.

Of course, the countering effect comes into play too. In all cases, people will come up against those souls wherein there lies a pre-existing conflict that needs to be fully resolved.

Counterbalancing is the key to all lifetimes. That is the canceling effect. Affections of the heart are wonderful and profound for the growth of a Soul over any lifetime. It is the most *underestimated thing* for humanity to understand; that the capacity of the heart is the capacity to heal. That as it is used, it grows stronger, that as we learn to love, we teach the Soul to grow and reach for more expansion of consequence. By that I mean, that all people could have everything in orderly fashion if they would simply listen to their hearts and be more human.

The human feelings are not to be clogged down, or trodden on. The feelings of the heart are to be honored and be honorable also. The baseline of the heart should be a communion of the soul with the mind and body. All relationships should be democratic and mankind could grow as a life force with this in mind; that as we think, we become. So, think love, think light and put light in all of your actions. Every day! In every given instance, let the soul therein reach out and sing its spirituality in all that it encounters.

As we work, let who we are truly come through. It should not be an ambiguous presentation with an essentially different personage emerging from behind closed doors. We should not be *two* people, ever! We should be one person and show that unity before all those that we meet on a daily basis.

Dishonesty of presentation is a big cause for trouble! All over the planet, people say one thing and are quite the opposite in the accountability of their activity. Deceit is the key to downfall. Trust begins as a heart issue. If we learn to trust from our childhood, then we view the worlds afar as friends, and there are no worlds apart because our hearts are joined and NOT separate in constitution. Only an understanding of this concept can make of humanity the giant it might become, a giant in respectability, a light force in discovery of itself. Discovery of itself, we say, is a magnificent thing, as we know that humanity will suffer without enlightenment. Humanity is in the process of attainment, addressing the needs of these higher wisdom goals, which will guide the Planet Earth along and *upward*.

And the heart is the key to fruition of all things there on the planet. Heart! It is the heart of man that must change and change radically from the attitude of selfishness, self- centeredness, indifference, lack of concern regarding others, and intolerance towards substantially different or competing forces representing diffusion from our respective viewpoints.

It is not enough that our differences will plow us under. This alone is, indeed, an understatement of the reality of observation of where we are in time. This attitude must change if the planet is to survive. Quickly, if mankind wants to equate all things in a material sense; the troubles of humanity will treble now as humanity has stepped into a world of higher technological advancement and soon that knowledge base will grow. It may not preserve humanity if the proper controls are not in place. To gain all that technological advancement on the planet is a dangerous thing, we say from this side, without the proper mental guidance for the use of that advancement.

This again is the same test that humanity did not do well with in "Atlantis!" The greatest civilization of all failed. Why? Because humanity lacked the ability to control itself; what it created; the technology that it created got away from the hands of the many into the hands of the few, and the few with the power used the forces to destroy their civilization

Soon, Planet Earth will reach this stage. Soon, we say, perhaps too soon, too few will have the power to destroy too many. This is why it is essential that we reach as many as will listen, **now**, Mrs. Lindsay. It is imperative that the people of the world heed the call against mass destruction, which could prevail against the whole of societies on the Planet Earth. ***We say nuclear power, unchecked, is a poisonous problem for humanity.***

Now the material concerns of many people on Planet Earth are leading them to be blinded in their daily lives, thinking that "the few", their leaders in power, will protect them. Such a lack of concern is reminiscent of the prevailing attitudes in Atlantis; we will not stand by and permit humanity to repeat this error of judgment without a fight from this side, the Spirit- side. We will fight with our thoughts and force them through to your side. We will go the distance with those that would hear us to bring our words to the forefront for consideration.

It is time to help and clearly, we say here, in this text, that the heart of humanity is "uneven and must rise to sufficiency" in order to save itself! The heart of humanity needs to be extended and then all will be protected with the best nature and the natural order coming from the heart, which has as the basic directive *the need to survive! To see the whole planet, survive! To see humanity, continue!*

And it is for all to be nourished, in what we give and in what we take. Change! The attitude needs to change to clear reception, with complete acknowledgement that there is a God that has given this planet to humanity with the clear directive to prosper and take care of the abundance that was initially given. We must live wisely with what was initially given to all, from the great Creator Himself, for all eternity, ***because it was good that He loved us and it was good that God spoke upon the chaos and created a heaven He called***... Planet Earth! ***And He did that for all*** of ***us! For all of us, everywhere!***

CHAPTER SEVEN

NEVER SUCH SWEET PARTING

THIS MISSION IS TO US A SACRED ONE. The journey ends on your side, Earth, and begins again on this side, Spirit, once the Soul has crossed over. You of Earth call this crossing death. We here know it is not death - but only a parting, - *a sweet parting.* *As* all that have lived *have gained.* All that have loved have increased their Soul capacity and will be further enriched for this next journey back into physicality when that is required. All there is to do then, once here, is to take up the life in the Spirit with the same practice of every moment existing, only the existing is here on this side without a physical body.

Now then we begin our new journey here and this mission to us is a sacred one. There, on Earth, you still do not understand, or I should say very few accept what I have just related as "fact": that there is absolutely life after death and then life after life. There is only "continuum." That is the point that I want to convey - only continuum!

This leads to a vast consideration? Then why are we in such a rush there, on Earth, to do everything so quickly? Why is the emphasis on such a deadlock of wits against the negativity towards growing old and aging? These are all-natural processes and there is nothing to fear, regarding these processes. This is the way that life has been growing, eon through eon. This works for humankind. This is the way and truth of it. There is no reason to panic there, on Earth, about everything. The truth, this truth, can set you free. If you can understand that and believe it, then this would gain everything for humankind as the desire to move will be replaced with a higher desire to move with sincerity and meaning with what we do on a daily basis. Also, it will give pause to so many that think now that they have only one lifetime and if they have not achieved what it is that they have sought to do, then they become despondent about that and will cease to grow or even reach for what it is they were about to accomplish because they fear their time has run out. **We could have a better start with this truth in the forefront**.

However, this truth is a high truth and is not being taught as such now. The reality of the truth on this Spirit-side needs to come to your side, the Earth plane. But? There is much resistance to it on the Earth at this time. It is a tricky subject, the subject of what we believe there.

Religion has so dominated the minds and hearts of everyone. God has been so loosely translated on Earth instead of being firmly understood as the *root* beginning of all things and as the *Absolute*, the *Providential One*, the immediate source of all. He has put the worlds in motion and then walked from it all to leave the rest of the genesis to us. Those that would see it that way will be better off than those that have never felt the presence of God in their lives. Humanity has the gift of God in its presence. It has the gift one to the other. The entire species has been blessed and we are the highest creation of God. We that have been human are the highest life form that God has created and He left us to continue to prevail with continuing on and to use what He initially gave to us, the goodness of all things that was primordial; He gave it to assure that humanity continues and that Planet Earth is a home that is healthy and beautiful for eons to come.

Everyone here has the privilege of existence! Everyone there, on Earth, that has come back into physicality comes with a mission: A directive to live and prosper; a directive that is the same directive that we were given from the beginning of creation.

This directive does not change. From lifetime to lifetime we return to Earth to live, love and grow up into wisdom consciousness as a society, individuals, and groups that will inhabit the Earth. These are the facts and humanity grows into acceptance of these truths, from lifetime after lifetime acquiring the skill of existence and eventually, at some point, the Soul seeks the higher ground and follows that lead to a higher cosmic line of thought.

Once that maturation begins, we step in and will assist that particular Soul, as that Soul will immediately stand out to us and we will give that Soul the additional time and attention One that breaks out like that will lead many others, as this is the nature of a leader. A leader will guide many through books of wisdom, such as this. This paves the way for our words, wisdom and information to be acquired there, on Earth, making it possible for many Souls to progress. So! We have quickened their pace to the Spirit life and that is a good thing. Whereas, many might *not* have stepped up to their next move, their next level, without these words in motion to inspire them.

It is a good thing that humanity understands the nature of preexistences is just that: preexistence. This makes all of us stop and think that we are being impressed with the wrong things right now, here at this time. If we could accept that the nature of our existence now has a tie to who we were before, that correlation would cause tremendous stimulation to the world's countering effects, one upon the other. It would change many people, almost instantly, because there would be so many wonderful possibilities then for so many. Also, it would make everyone consider all actions, knowing what they are creating is important and the creation of their thoughts has a correlation in their deeds. And so on.

But, for now, the practical side of this is that life is a continuum. Whether humanity there, on Earth, accepts it does not change the fact that it is so. The principal of it is alive and working well. That it is not appreciated nor understood to be a practical application, does not change the fact that it is in motion. Do you see how that translates? *It is!* That this is not understood does not change the fact that *it is*. What is in operation continues to function and maintain its operation, and that is the cosmic law in governance of the worlds and the universes. God put it all in motion. As we grow through these life forms and lifetimes, we will learn to respect what and why He has put it all in motion, this way. It is the directive of all peoples now, just to grasp this higher truth, which is moving, softly, at least softly, even if they are not capable yet of grasping it with both hands. There is a footing someplace. And we say it could be a simple beginning for some, just with the mind rolling through the pages of this book, with no prior readings on this subject elsewhere. At least we will try. We will try, to be sure.

Now about this crossing, it is "sweet" and there is nothing to fear. Each Soul is greeted here. All are welcomed and assisted on this side, the side of Spirit. No one, *no one* stands alone at the crossing from the passage of life on Earth to life in the Spirit. So, all of you still in the physical must relax about death. As you have nothing to do except, do it, transition, when it is your turn, again, to do so. Sweetness greets all!

The judgment that so many religions teach does happen, but not as is written. The Soul judges itself here, when it gets here, back to the Spirit world. And, the art of regular reviewing is a wise thing to learn to do for ourselves, every day, as we live, to end up *reviewing what we did within that day.* And if we created "unevenness" for someone else, then we need to correct ourselves, *as soon as possible*, with that person or that situation.

It is as simple as that. Be good, and be *immediate with your good*. Say what you mean. Mean what you say. Live with firmness and integrity. Take time for everyone and be conscious of the fact *that you have time.* You have time for everything and everyone! So, what's the rush? The rush needs to stop. **You need to slow down and love more and cherish more and give to each other the joy of hearts that humanity is so capable of.**

Hate is a thing to despise! Learn to step away from hate and challenge all who think that hate is a good characteristic. It is not. Teach tolerance and learn to debate openly with sincerity of heart and respect at the baseline of any debate. All are equal and equal time should be given to all. Listen to each other and extend an accord of thoughts to each other.

Open exchanges of ready thoughts are not to end in hateful debate. Men and women need to speak with voices that are pitched to a lower key. Distress is causing much needless unhappiness to the human Soul now upon Planet Earth. It needs to stop and people need to slow up the train that would hobble them. Why continue at that frightening pace? Whatever for? Slow down and *do smell the roses and love each other today.*

There is a message in a garden. Look at the garden and what do you see? So many beautiful things that are waiting to be simply appreciated! Stop and observe. How many things can you count that you can see in a garden? How many of those things are large? Now how many are small? What is most important? Would you consider it as beautiful or as lovely, if all of the large things were missing? Now imagine that all of the small things were missing, with just the large things there. And then imagine that the birds would not come, if there were not flowers for them to touch and gather what they need from the flowers. Now imagine the bees coming and adding their part to this lovely garden. Mother nature has a full plan and it is not complete without the large things in order and the small things there too. All of it is important. And life is best like that. Think of it as a full view and any disparity that one experiences, should be thought of within that picture as being a *necessary part.* At first, it may not be easily understood that weeds are part of the garden, but every road has its weeds. It is not all flowers as we go upon the road.

Weeds need to be tended as we go; *we shoulder the burdens of our adversities*. We cannot run from them. We must learn to overcome all obstacles in our stride and that stride should be easily made. We should not constantly be stressing about our daily journey to work and from work and all the people, places and things in between.

It is wise to understand that we should learn to love all and ourselves within the "all" as we live out our lifetimes. If we can learn to look at it this way, *we will learn to become masters*. As we learn to reflect this higher understanding, we will grow in our ability to choose wisely and use our resources and our times well.

Our family mates, our children and business associates and partners will learn that we can be counted on and rightly so. Because we will be disciplined in our approach to our duties, respect our duties and complete them as they are presented, with a cheerful attitude. Not an attitude that is always drawn to negativity and complaints as we move along with what it is that we must do in life.

Cooperate with the Spirit in all things. This Spirit surrounds us at all times. We need only to understand that there is nothing and no other human force to go against! *We are the only one that is holding us up*. The rest are memories that are stored, which need to be deleted from our consciousness. **We need to outgrow that which is thought to be holding us back.**

We need to grow away from those thoughts and replace them with thoughts that would allow us to move quickly in discerning that we are in charge of our immediate circumstances, our immediate lives. And then this life becomes a journey that is welcomed and appreciated.

OH! Such a joy to live in the human body once it is understood that life is meant to be a thing of beauty. All can have the rest and peace that they seek. We must learn to listen and make a better world with each other. Do not resort to old "knots", constricting beliefs or constructs that we have created – imagery and descriptions of disparity and discomfort - images that would restate our lack of victory, or loss of virtue that was yesterday. Today, we come again to live and change into better people with a grander vision at our helms. Steer for that grander vision of yourself and make it come about. Never give in to less. We are meant to grow in all things and to bring others to our story of growth as well. We will, all, come about on this fabulous journey to love and to life.

CHAPTER EIGHT

WHEN WE MEET WE LOVE

In the beginning it was man and woman as the two co- creators with the genius of God, the ultimate Creator.

NOW IN THE BEGINNING, God created Adam and Eve or man and woman, for the sole purpose of beginning His generations of humankind. It was a very good thing that He did so. Because the evolution of the universe depended on God's greatest creations, most intelligent offerings, man and his mate, female, to populate the worlds and successfully bring about life forms out of the chemical chaos existent at the time of the nexus of creativity, the beginning of all things universal.

And so, it came to be, that God created the *attraction*, the basic attraction of man to his mate, female. And so, it was that man discovered her in his latent stage of pubescence and found her to be most delightful in her sensual nature, bringing him much pleasure in and at the time of sexual rapture.

Also, she became his soul-mate on all other issues, having herself, her own plane of existence, much the same as her mate, man, only different within the characteristics that opposites require in polarity, to balance each other effectively.

"Female" was designed to bring pleasure to the male and assist him in all other matters of necessities, during their necessary life spans upon Planet Earth, which are many lifetimes over the course of enveloping eons. Your measurement of Earth refers to eons, for which we say are actually "rounds" of existence corresponding to the uplifting stages of planetary consciousness and spirituality of civilizations.

And so, it happened that over the eons of time, the human race improved and grew into its present stage of advancement, open communication, with detailed sophisticated systems of transmission and with the human intelligence required to operate these systems. This opposed the past stages of human development wherein dross, gross ignorance and lack of ability to comprehend even the most basic things in life on the Planet Earth was the general level of existence. The improvements have been dramatic and have come about as part of the plans in mankind's ascendancy.

This ability to comprehend brings us to the present because without it, man could not have progressed to this stage in the technological whirlwind. This stage is the ascendancy of consciousness wherein mankind will engage himself beyond what he is doing currently. And it is this very ability that I want to expand upon in this chapter, as it is at the front and center of the vanguard of human thought, which comprehension will guide all of humanity going forward.

It is a simple thing, and it is necessary for survival of humanity, the desire to LOVE each other. This "will", that will prevail, assures continued access to the communication with God and his creativity in design. This determination and strength of character allows man to accept the down- pouring of information that will come to him through the natural course of his divinity, incrementally increasing through to the next stage of ascendance.

Free will is at work now and we will sponsor many couples before they come together. Not all couples will be sponsored, however. But those that we know are destined to lead, we will assure their coming together for mating purposes so that the group, humanity at large, can benefit from the primary force of their leading authority which will be required. From some males, and some selective females, order is assured and allows for the continuance of the finer qualities of the races. The guardians bringing these couples together, assures that they will meet their destined mates, strengthening the survival qualifies of the human race over the course of time and matter.

And when we meet, we LOVE. There is no greater assurance that mankind will continue with his best efforts than to know that he maintains his ability to love, to extend love and to receive love. Love is the greatest force in the universe. It is the binding force for humanity. It is a blessed union from the Creator of the universe. It is the preferred state of mind for all people on this planet. It is the hardest, however, to achieve due to many things that we intend to discuss here.

This is in no way to put down, or consider less worthy, the other choices of vocation, instead of marriage and procreation, which exist for humanity.

Saints are always needed and welcomed! The ascetic life, devoted totally to the love of God, the holy Creator, is a most noble choice for the Soul when it is ready to lead that life. Helping self and humanity with the Soul's spirituality by example of generosity of spirit, love, and holy guidance by virtue is implicit in the habit worn by nuns, priests and other types of clergy.

Sometimes, the Soul chooses a solitary life on its own. Many times, great reflection is given to self-interests during this type of life, wherein this span becomes the necessary breather from former lives, which lacked cohesiveness, which brings peace and quietude required for full self-expression, and focused creation of excellence in a particular field of study, as an example of what can be achieved with this level of directed energy. All life choices regarding vocation, should be considered with purpose and all energy with directiveness, which can make holy a life, when vision and intensity are applied to progressing upward with pure dedication on our journey. It is up to the entity to make it so!

It is a *generosity of spirit* that encourages love upon this Planet Earth. It is to the highest order of things, that we all learn the power of love and make the commitment to love each other in our daily lives. It will change all other things on this plane of consciousness for the good. It is achievable now, more than ever - you have so much to give to each other there, on Earth.

Know that there is no limitation to this thing called LOVE! It is inexhaustible! It is infinite in its power. And it is this power that the human race needs to tap into. It will take us away from negativity, easily setting our feet upon the path to "upward progress of all things that are positive"!

Fear cannot withstand in the face of Love. Love is stronger than everything else that exists on the Earth. It is the *strongest weapon in the universe*. It is the one weapon, wherein peace can provide for all, *all* which is essential to existence. Yet, application of this principle takes mastery of self and this takes time and reflection.

We will learn that this state of mind is most conducive to achieving the brotherhood of all races upon the Planet Earth, at this time. It is an achievable thing…***Peace***. Peace on this planet. Yes, it is a good thing and all must strive to get to this level of existence, *peacefulness for all. Love and kindness prevailing, worldwide!*

Peace! How is this possible for all, you would ask of me, Master Rama? *I will tell you that it is the very possibility of the thing that is so thrilling.* To think that we can get "there", to PEACE, is awesome even to me. It begins with small steps put into certain motion as we go *forward with confidence* into these various lifetimes, each lifetime *improving* from the last one lived.

And with each lifetime, we gain better control over the use of our innate faculties. The instrument of the Soul, the essential being, becomes more educated through the years of trials, learning to adapt more quickly to its new circumstances within its current body vessel. This sets the pace of possible achievement higher than the previous lifetimes.

Each new lifetime builds from the former total achieved and retained by the Higher-Self, in the Akashic records, for use in future lives.

Relationships are key to driving the new vehicle along the road of life. The role of the *mother* is exceedingly important in any new lifetime, as she is the first nurturer, the first natural accord, the lover and protector of the child. The father is secondary to the mother, during the initiation of primary stage child development, having completed his main function in the seeding of the child, the actual act of fathering.

The traits of the child will be guided and nurtured through the integral love of both parents. Their natural gifts, "love bearing", being the greatest gift to be shared with their newborn, over the course of a lifetime of bonding, creating crucial focus and foundation for their offspring.

This is where the age of the Soul comes into play. We are not all at the same level regarding this matter. There are Souls that are very old, having gained much wisdom from many lives prior and there are Souls that are young in experience and will, most likely, have to wait many lifetimes to learn how to gain mastery over the instrument, the human body.

This is why it is essential to the development of humanity, to have strong, sage, human leadership at the top, mixed within the population on the Earth at any one time. This assures the upward trend overall and staves off the possibility of downward spirituality and demoralization of humanity, generally speaking. The sage Souls assure tranquility for Planet Earth, enough to stabilize it and push it out further with what it must gain overall. Parents and children will have karmic ties that will encourage advancement.

Prior love, which was established in previous life waves, will be a basis for an innate foundation in any new lifetime. This is why family relationships are so important to all reentries and why we work so diligently, on this side, to coordinate possible correlations in the plan overview in order to provide the best likelihood of success to the individual Souls, returning to take up life again, in the human form.

The human body must be controlled effectively in order to achieve the balance required to use the mind, to train the innate qualities of intelligence that are responsible for the higher functioning of humanity. As more people achieve this level of intelligent control, then we will move forward faster, as more will participate in the advancements of the scientific fields **in which we are destined to change the focus of the world.**

When we meet, we LOVE. That is the accord to be strengthened time after time in life form. This is the message that cannot be repeated often enough. Learning to love is learning to grow and *let go* of our basic motivation, which is usually self-serving, coming from self-centeredness. This is key to moving forward to greatness.

Picking up the pace to love will be the very best thing that we can do to make a steady move to peace on the planet. With love comes the ability to care and to make the ultimate goal - just the satisfaction in knowing that we do all things in the name of love, increasing the nobility of the human race.

Love is the ultimate answer to all things! Love of self, love of family, love of community, love of all things upon the Earth. Love! Of God's planet, love of all that He gave to us in our worlds to enjoy, breathe in strength from and gain pure love from the Godhead and the desire to join with Him in all matters.

And *to protect our love with more love…to believe and trust, not* always in defense of our newly found possessions or worshiping our accrued savings; all that is material is mutable. Therefore, only love and other essential qualitative metaphysical gains will move forward to be added to Soul essences, which are gained in summary statement on this side, the world of Spirit, after each lifetime is concluded. All will come back over here into pure Spirit for "sorting" after each lifetime.

The magnitude of import regarding the matter of how much we increase our overall ability and desire *to love* in any lifetime is huge. *There is almost no quantity that would be considered too much! This is better understood by the saints -* for these Souls are saints because they understood the quality of LOVE and mastered the need to give of self to such a degree that their very images were transformed to reflect the Creator's larger vision of the world he loved and gave to us. We call this His "majestic eye" the all knowingness and all being of ALL that is grand within the true nature of the world.

There is still much that I want to say regarding the matter of comprehension that man has achieved, because as we can comprehend so we can move ahead. And each generation of humankind is able to perceive a little more than the last. Each generation will translate the down pouring of information to the best of its ability and its ability will improve as it grows in spiritual quality.

By spirituality, we are referring to the *overall condition of spirit* and not the choice of religion that any Soul will take up for that particular lifetime. These are two different aspects. The one is the aspect of church going which is tied usually to traditional family matters of preference and passed along from the parents to the children. Usually, the aspect of church studies will change from lifetime to lifetime tied into the family preference, already established prior to the Soul arriving into that family. It is a matter of choice and all will experience *many* types of religions during the life spans.

The second reference is one to the spiritual essence, the Soul that transcends any given religious aspect chosen for selective participation by the entity in any one lifetime.

Intolerance of any "religious aspect" is intolerance for all. The point is to study wherein one lies. The Godhead is the same for all and only the choice of church to study with needs to be made. But the lessons will move around the central understanding, as many of the understandings of religions today have more in common than previously.

Broad based religious attitudes exist in the world today, one side by side with the other. Extreme religions such as exist in the Middle Eastern cultures; will take many more years to broaden the scope of tolerance. In *the meantime, the rest of the world will experience a return to acceptance and tolerance of many types of religions, all over the planet, co-existing without trouble.*

When we meet, we LOVE - there is no grander statement than that. It is to the highest order of the existence of man that he loves and stays in love with all that he creates, with all that he surrounds himself with, day in and day out. To find delight in all he does and all those that he encounters day in and day out. To face the world with a positive, systematic approach and lead all those that he works with to this feeling of promise and trust in something larger than himself which is about to unfold.

This eminent trusting Spirit in advance of action will make it come alive within him and within the structure of what it is he does. And it does not matter what his occupation is, *as all occupations can be holy if they are offered to God with dignity every day.*

All have the same opportunity for greatness once they understand the point of reflection to be meditated on. That point is the face of God, which is available to all, from all perspectives of view. The eye of the beholder is blessed from the beginning having his own key to his own visions of the Creator. In simply beholding the *very thought* of the Creator, the Creator lifts one up as one thinks of him. If one were to meditate daily, on just that, it would create a significant change for the better within the basic personality and demeanor of the subject. What we think about daily, daily we create. Mental energy is energy, which builds upon itself.

There are no weighted objects that are holding us back in stride upon Planet Earth. It is mankind that burdens himself with what it is he does within his daily life and the obligations he involves himself with and enslaves himself under.

Making deities of "things" that would enslave us is not wisdom. There is no wisdom achieved in the majesty of four walls of gold. It would be a far greater use of time to meditate on the Godhead for a lifetime sitting under a tree looking and listening for Him, the Creator to arrive or waiting for His emissaries to announce His arrival or visitation. Of course, this world would decry otherwise and therein lays the rub and the rude awakening.

When we meet, we LOVE. There is nothing finer than that and nothing finer than the ability to ascertain the quality within that statement. This rule is golden…Love thy neighbor as thyself. That is a golden rule and so it goes that man must find himself on many planes before he is complete and full. Patience is truly a virtue within this consideration.

Comprehension of what it is we give meaning to is key to finding better ways to live, better uses of our time, resources, and energies. There is much wisdom in thinking like that and changing our attitudes where required to fit within this adage:

Love thy neighbor as thyself!

When we meet, we Love…So Love! Peace be with you as you go
with that thought and as I end this Chapter on LOVE!

CHAPTER NINE

SEASONS AND LIFETIMES

TO BEGIN WITH seasons and lifetimes have much in common and these things relate to regular changes that are predictable by the human eye and/or other human perceptions and faculties. These regular changes are noted, listed, standardized on records as cyclical occurrences, predicated upon the fact that they can be observed as occurring on Earth each season. In repeating fashion, these phenomena can be observed as lasting in duration, in similar intervals to previous experiences realized in comparable historical periods of time, establishing trend lines over the time they are observed.

It can be said that spring is the beginning of all the seasons and perhaps the most beautiful one to behold. In the springtime the meadows are lush with the new growth of green grasses. Suddenly! The wild flowers are appearing in the grass, popping up through the green grass with splendor in a wonderful palette of colors for the human eye to behold. *It is pure joy* to watch this happening each year as "Mother Nature" weaves her magical spell again!

Is it any wonder that we all look forward to springtime after our cold winters of discontent? Weather has always been an element that has challenged humanity for eons. Weather has been a problem since the beginning of times. To know these predictable schedules of seasonal changes was an important point of observable tracking for humankind, trying to master climatic changes and environments.

Successful farming was imperative for survival of the populace. Understanding the waterways was crucial to moving around on the Planet Earth; sailing from one small point to another, learning to find each other and what existed beyond one's established area.

Compassing through chartered waters was most important to negotiating tides with success. Mapping became important. Civilizations depended upon talented discoverers, who used their early methods of cartography to help them remember lands and topographic characteristics of the lands, which they had visited. It was very important to gain an understanding of nearby countries, possible allies, and possible enemies. Force soon arrived upon the Earth. Man found the knowledge to heat metals and mold them into "things". Athens and Greece became points of supremacy, using their weapons freely to gain domination upon the land in ancient times.

Understanding weaponry became necessary as man gained knowledge of personal power and the requirement *to defend* oneself from one's enemies, *or so it has always seemed, the need to remain DEFENSIVE, ready with our weapons! In the minds of many men, throughout time on the Planet Earth, this has been deemed a primary requirement.*

Strength, physical strength in numbers, became something the early kings demanded. All civilizations mounted themselves with fury to gain military supremacy and to match their wits with each other. War became a common occurrence and was viewed as such. These things were passed down to the children of warriors and then a new crop of warriors arrived in time to outlive their fathers and die anew upon a battlefield; fighting for supremacy or meager survival against it, accosted by a stronger approaching, physically encroaching force. Force became the rule of the day. Standing armies were attending the daylight dressed for war and warlords to prevail!

Country after country took on this same "attitude" and humanity never looked back! Time has never seen otherwise upon this Planet Earth! War is still considered a common event, naturally *repeating as any season*, as the nature of mankind has been recorded. History repeats itself, with new titles of new wars, in new places, in new books of history and politics.

*It is **thought, even now as we write,** by so many in charge, at the helms of the military, world-wide, that it will always be so; war and the readiness for war, are deemed daily duties to perform upon the Earth, by standing armies all over the planet.* This is not a debatable need, is the thought of many. It is considered folly to fight with this academic principle. The BELIEF IN WAR prevails! The best and the brightest in high places agree: War is a necessary evil, sometimes! And if there is a 1 percent chance of it coming, we must be ready for it, to WIN! To survive - to prevail!

Aggressive characteristics of this tribal warfare way of thinking have always existed for humanity, as the *lack of concern* for the Spiritual has always been a constant, contributing factor in the rebirthing and repetition of what has not been settled in the minds of humankind; honoring all things that are tangible and as we see, *still being unable to honor the consciousness from within.*

This is an eternal upward spiral for humanity and a struggle even now, finding civilities, while using sophisticated methods of warfare and yet still the mindset of ignorance towards the Spirit!

Existence here on Planet Earth is still so difficult for so many because we lack the ability to comprehend the necessity of Spiritual balance, inherent in the successful process of human growth, which is Spiritual at the core! ***Growth of the Spirit is not a drawback, in fact, we say, it is the only way to go forward!***

Humanity has struggled with assessing the seasons and prevailing winds. To know the conditions of these things became imperative to all that would go abroad by sailing vessels in the times of old. All commerce then depended so much on the seas.

Now in your world so much depends on what is delivered by air and even everyday people fly around this world today by taking a craft, a marvelous airplane of conveyance. And people globetrot in record numbers, all depending on the ability to do so, that then being governed primarily by personal wealth or business hierarchy and positioning.

The global reach upon Planet Earth at this time is significant. It is no longer a closed world, inaccessible due to distancing, in terms of continental divides and oceans of blue.

Wireless communication, through satellite, has linked all of the civilizations upon the Earth together. This has created a stage of vacuous discontent and creation of concurrent jealousies, as other parts of the less organized, less civilized world, view the United States of America and the other cultures, with constraint.

Therein lies the cognizant realization of the differences in wealth and power that exist around the globe. These differentials being observed as huge and outstanding differences to the naked eye, audible differences expressed in educated values of comparison, reported in newsworthy fashion to audiences that will hear on a daily basis, tuning in for regular television or radio updates.

The common folk of so many of these other nations do not share in the privileges of freedom and all the good that comes to these countries due to a wide distribution of wealth and power. We call this plan that works so well - Democracy. And people that live there, in lands of freedom, are called "free people"!

The United States of America and England have gone the distance with each other, many times throughout history, side by side, because they share in this common theme of "freedom and democracy" in their respective countries and have fought in order to preserve these privileges, which their cultures must have to survive.

Remaining skeptical, however, are the lesser countries that lack these cohesive powers, as their countries have not yet set up such a geo-political economic system. The people at these locations in the world suffer the consequences of this lack of development, lack of sponsorship and lack of freedom, as freedom needs a solid law and order presence to prevail and create a dependable infrastructure to survive.

We have spoken in previous chapters about *war and peace*. We have spoken about the hardest things to overcome in the world that cause the build-up and prelude to war: *intolerance, inequalities and greed*. We have also talked in previous chapters about fear and ignorance. It is no mistake to repeat these powerful points in this chapter, as they do indeed tie into the theme of seasons and lifetimes, repeating, again and again; growth is indeed a distant drummer.

Because of our fears we are repeating many life lessons again. Fear is a constant that will drive humanity back to Earth for resolution of conflict. Make no mistake, what we fear we will repeat until we learn to balance ourselves better. Balancing may take many lifetimes as fear retards the necessary growth in the area that needed healing and mending.

Many times, people cannot complete even one full life lesson value in one lifetime. Just as in a season, it takes repeating to clear out some trends and tendencies. Bad habits are pernicious. People are like that also, difficult and stubborn, *in obvious need of proper subordination of self- traits*, behaviors, and emotional insecurities; acting out through instability, creating personality disorders, dysfunction, addiction, and many other types of personal problems that cause havoc and unhappiness.

When proper subordination of self-traits is begun, however, this establishes, immediately, in the psyche of the Spirit, a new trend of change, which will properly set in motion discovery of the correct correlating resolution to the problem. Then *elimination* of the character flaw can begin. Through the application of the solution, the underlying trend that needs to be changed *can be changed,* therein eliminating the bad habit, forever, in the residual memory bank of the entity. Overcoming ourselves is part of the growth process! Onward and upward!

Understanding, alone, is not a galvanization process and these things are thought forms that create and are literally fluid, ripe with the possibility of negativity or constructiveness in action.

Understanding *that we have choices* is the key to developing *strong wills,* which wills create many possible cornerstones upon which much good can be established. Havoc and disorder are no longer the weight of the day, the weight that we are carrying lifetime after lifetime, burdening ourselves over and over again with thoughts of defeat in all matters and deficient consequences in our experiences in life.

Without a strong will, our minds cannot withstand the pressure to the pull of laziness, disinclination and lack of ambition, which are the things that the human form will succumb to, left to its own devices, unchecked, and unsupervised by a wisdom mind.

Patiently, progress is made to lift the hearts and minds of humanity upward, as it is coming of age wherein real, next- step, highly technological advancement can be achieved, propelling mankind into outer space travel, the likes of which are not possible now.

Again, we are reaching that point where humanity is getting ready for the job of spiraling upwards, towards higher ground in thought form.

These thoughts are coming from the stream of knowledge, the down pouring of blessings from this side that we have said previously, is a naturally occurring constant, going on all the time. It is as natural as the indwelling of Spirit, sunny and bright, always provident!

When this down pouring is aggressively and positively accessed by humanity, the miracle-like realization in discovery and invention can occur. Through meditation, prayer, and sincere application of discipline to these higher accords of Spirit, union with mind and body coalesce creating heart and mind right action as a way of life. These conditions can set in motion the creation of needed intensity of thought, which can allow for that individualized Spirit to bring in information for humanity that will change the world and greatly improve life for all on the Spaceship Earth.

And it is wise to remember that this is a space ship. Planet Earth is but a small planet within the universe, which universe, we say, is full of beautiful, nascent, small planets awaiting initial genesis.

Many other planets in the solar systems are inhabited, genesis having begun long ago, but these cultures have not reached the extremes of their intelligence either, that would embark them along the path, leading to the knowledge that they need to ascertain for vast scientific discovery and exploration in space.

Once ascertaining the knowledge in declarative form, root solutions for the problems of advanced understanding of manipulation of gravity, fuels, and materials required for galactic travel, can be obtained. To which we say here, in Spirit, that this knowledge is waiting now to be discovered, but for which we say further, mankind *is not ready to handle the discoveries* that the knowledge would naturally produce, taken to its fullness in application.

As we have said prior, we will not bring forward next-step, technological understandings, until the cultures of the planets are ready. It is too risky to do otherwise. We are not in the business of setting up humanities for destruction. ***This is not the message - this is never the goal from this side***. We patiently wait for humanity to mature in mind and wisdom base. Eons we will wait patiently, assisting in this path to progress.

Warfare is not a *proper end result* for the scientific data that we send through to your Planet- Earth. These trend lines on your planet need to be observed and corrected, as quickly as possible, as they set in motion new lines of demarcation between countries, which lines lead and lend intensely to further seriousness in war upon your planet, the Planet Earth.

And these possibilities of forthcoming war upon your planet bring us much concern. Concerns were also expressed for the great Atlantis that reached a similar point. For which we say, we were too late to rescue that changeover, leading into mass destruction. We would like to repeat that our mission is to promote advancement and move humanity away from the similar problems, which led up to the destruction of the great Atlantis. Technological gifts which spread to the use of the negativity of the force on a planet, can lead to a level of destructiveness, to the magnitude, we say, that can take out an entire "round" of evolving people, evolving Souls.

To lose this Planet Earth to that end would be a far greater loss than Atlantis, as the populace now upon this planet is much larger and the scale of harmfulness, at the peak of nuclear obliteration, would be; tantamount to a huge blast going many, many miles into an infusion - blending throughout the waves of universal tides; These waves of contamination-distributed combination of energy particles -will set in motion upon the other parts of the universe, releasing in unison, a negative charge; that would affect the balance of the universe and create the instant need of an immediate response to counterbalance the effects, therein causing a destructive-like series of events in the other worlds too!

This is the larger concern, not just for your planet; in the event of destruction, the reception of destructive particles that would, most likely, go into circulation upon an explosion and destruction in your world, Planet Earth, would also produce devastating effects throughout the Universe.

We cannot say this too clearly here, in print. That is, Polarity, in its negative force, creates this imminent possibility, which we wish to bring to the attention of your world, so that all will do what is necessary *to avoid such a collision course with concentrated, negative energy fields.*

Do not allow these negative trend lines to grow. Address them now and prevent war. Do all that is necessary to avoid war and killing each other. Do these things well, every day and the Spiritual guides will assist with all other necessities of sustenance.

As we see it, this Planet Earth is one of the leading candidates to receive our sponsorship towards galactic possibilities, if only we can get through this negative trend, reduce it, and put it down, completely.

Scholarly efforts could then begin on the positive side; efforts that could bring to the Earth a lush state of happiness and abundance, which cannot now be imagined - the human mind, body and Soul in true natural order and balance. Such an achievement is what we say is possible, but for now, it is one day at a time, addressing our smaller, immediate issues that will teach us what we must do to address our larger issues, further down the line to maturation.

Peace and harmony begin with the individualized Soul achieving for itself and then sharing that peace and harmony with others throughout life. These things are to be shared amongst each other: love, honor and obedience to the universal codes of fairness and brotherhood of all that exist, as all that exists must co-exist with each other, side by side.

It is the obligation of all Souls that live on the Planet Earth now, to come to a union in heart, mind and body, which promotes the spirit of togetherness and *harmonizing solutions*. It is now imperative that the peoples of Earth speak to each other with one voice, the voice of peace and harmony. This voice promotes a total healing to the problems of Earth.

War is never the solution. War only induces further aggravated assaults; one nation eventually achieving revenge, in some way, upon the other, to avenge lost civilizations.

And it goes on and on in that way. The character traits of humankind need to improve greatly, so that much good can now come to the entire world.

We are waiting for the pace to pick up. It is time for all to see that the planet needs to be lifted up. Only through a "joint effort" of all countries upon the Earth is it possible to solve the overlying problems of the world.

The indwelling Spirit of each individual is capable of leading itself; if each Soul would only give heed to its internal directives that come through, everywhere, every day. It is not possible for one **not** to be guided. Although many, we say most, *do not understand* that this guidance is coming to them daily, or that acknowledging this guidance would make them more likely to be governed by rightness of thought and action, which would lead them to *all* material things that are required for sustenance.

Abundance is the natural order of things. "Lack" is a hard mindset, when it is backed with practiced, daily belief in its existence. What we choose to believe is up to us. Which would you rather believe in, "abundance"? or "lack"? As you go about your daily business of today, study yourself in your actions and ask yourself this, *"abundance"* or **"lack"**, who am I? Am I in this body? If so, am I *"abundance"*? or am I **"lack"**? This is a point of meditation.

I hope that you find yourselves abundant, as the Spirit is *truly,* in pure essence, tranquil, and ready to give and share what it owns with all other Souls; wisdom of the ages. So, mote it be!

CHAPTER TEN

"DESTINY - A CORE ISSUE FOR ALL"

TO BEGIN WITH, we are going to look at "destiny", not the subject of pre-destination. Let us separate out the two, as the two are completely different. First, pre-destine refers to the human condition, determination on its own, as if the choice could be made. The second is destiny, which in fact is the choice, set from the astral plane level, from here in this realm of consciousness. It is, in fact, set by the Counsel and the Soul going back into human form, before the Soul actually re-enters.

Now, the choice of destiny is worked out with the aspirant who is to return to Earth. Based on *two major things*, destiny considerations begin thus: individual, remaining karma, in summary from all previous lives wherein work is required is reviewed and the major life lessons that the Soul wishes to work on in the next incarnation. Further considerations are made based on previous talents acquired and the bank of achievements already established by the Soul.

These Akashic records are held in summary, in the aggregate, after each lifetime and during the actual lifetime while in the physical world of matter. These information files are held, in essence, by the human brain center. This data is controlled through the operation system, the Higher-Self or the Oversoul, whichever you want to call it, as they are the same. We are Spirit essence before we become physical again. We are Spiritual essence again, once our current lifetime is completed, and we have left the physical body and returned to the Spirit-side, the side from which I dictate today. This is the basic procedure.

We have said previously, that after each lifetime, the Over-soul gathers all the remaining "good"; keeps it, stores it in the system, which is a succinct synopsis of a combination of language and pictures, so that it is easily translated when it needs to be pulled up, opened, and referenced by us; if the Soul needs to visit the database with us in a dual review, which review occurs often here, for various reasons. It is one of the teaching methods that we use here, Spirit-side, for the purposes of analytical study.

We have so many wonderful things to say about our teaching methods here, in the Spirit, and that definitely will be another Chapter. But this Chapter is about the subject at hand, destiny and destiny versus free will, as there seems too often to be a disconnect between the two. By the way, we do not see from here, Spirit-side, that there is a conflict between these two things such as one versus the other.

Destiny is in fact a core issue for all, as all must refer to the "choices" that they have made earlier in their previous lives, which then leads them to the next point of destiny. There is the destiny of parents, career choices and the other main theme; destined lovers. The patterns established involve all three parts of a life.

Parental destiny… I would like to open this file first, as it is extremely important. As our fathers and mothers are the core circle of our survival, so it matters greatly whom it is that we chose to come back through.

And we often return through the same family connections and often, will reverse positions. Sometimes we were the *fathers* for our next fathers; sometimes they were our brothers and sisters from a previous lifetime and/or close relatives. There is a reason for returning to them for the re-experience with life…LOVE, the love connection. It cannot be stressed enough, that this is the *strongest connection*, which exists for humankind. So, I would have to say that this link, the "love connection", is the one that truly binds the Soul on re-entry.

The lessons that we learn are very similar to the previous life lessons but, with established parental connections from previous lives, that next new love connection, can be a **greater love** and help the Soul reemerge within the rest of its life in a **greater sense** and with a **greater desire** for success and achievement towards a life lesson not completed on the last try. We may return to try again, if it is strong enough, *the pull* to a certain thing by which to learn and express our talents through.

Even our physical attributes have been saved in the Akashic files. It is likely that we will choose a similar body style and personal look to what we have had before. It is often surprising to us here, Spirit-side, that people will pick out the "same" features again and again. Even though they can change and request better vehicles for re-entry, oftentimes they don't, seemingly content with what they had previously or not caring to put more into the art of creating beautiful bodies or beautiful images required for this process of creation, which is of mental bearing before it is materialized in a true physical nature.

What can be started, as a seed, to germinate must be sponsored by the Soul in actuality once it lives! Only on the Earth plane can the seeds take life. As here, in Spirit, we have no bodies and no place to plant the seeds of destiny, as they all come into fruition on your side, within the world of physicality, if and when they come. Here we are 100 percent spirituality; we have no life forms and could not use them here, Spirit-side, if we had them. The ethos here, on these planes, will not support physical life.

We simply cannot tell you that your bodies are not important, but to us, with ethereal bodies, we feel these are superior to your human bodies because we do not have to support them all the time with physical care and nourishment. Yet here, in Spirit, we derive many of the pleasures that come through the body as expressed on Earth. Here pleasures are expressed differently, in a spiritual consciousness, which is very satisfying.

Also, we have love here, in the Spirit world and people to love all around us, all the time. As we are governed here by thought power, we think our way to everything and everyone, almost in an instantaneous fashion.

Parents are, indeed, important and will help the child grow and become able to sustain itself in the world. So then, our parents will give us many things and the most **important thing that they will give us *is their love*** and we have said that earlier.

Now, to the matter of career choices…

Usually, the Soul will seek to reenter with a very strong primary career/vocational interest. There will be secondary choices and interests as well, but the Soul will have a definite leaning towards a particular gift, which the Soul has chosen to express once returning to Planet Earth. This choice having been established well in advance, before the Council, which council helps the Soul to choose from the review what it wants to express further on the Earth plane. And that survey of gifts and summary of lifetimes is something that we do here, in the Spirit; before the Soul goes over, back to Earth, to start its next physical lifetime. We have stated these things before in previous chapters. So mote it be.

This is all part of the processing that occurs and as haphazard as it may sound, it is not. In particular it is a very detailed analysis that happens over here, Spirit-side, as it is the primary interest here to help the Soul do better on the next round into physicality. The goal of the journey during lifetimes is to prepare the Soul for reaching the level of perfection, the balancing of all experiences, where it will do its best to obtain the higher planes of existence, which are beyond the physical form. But this usually takes many lifetimes before the Soul will even *begin* to reach for that opportunity, the opportunity to move up, out of a physical body to existence in a Spirit body, beyond the Earth plane.

Until then, we do not rush these matters. There is no need to rush, as rushing will only hamper further development. It is up to the Soul to make its own way, time and time again. There is no easy path, one that is absolutely assured on your side, Planet Earth. All that we can do is do our best here to guide the Soul before it comes back to the Earth plane and help it with understanding that *"it is in charge of pursuing its own point of destiny."*

Destiny and free will, these two things are created equally. The two things are similar and yet dissimilar, as we will see. Let me explain here, within this text. It is a complicated thing but a necessary thing. As what good would it be to create one without the other? As the growth of the destiny depends so much on the growth of the Soul! And the Soul cannot make proper progress towards anything worthwhile until it learns *to discipline* itself through the *use of its free will.* The time is well spent then, when the Soul *learns that it must put time into what it chooses to develop for itself, whether that is a career/ vocation interest or otherwise.*

The more determination that the entity affords for itself, the more the possibility exists that the Soul will make stride in the area of a career choice, which it wishes to impress upon its own individualized operation system. The Oversoul will aid and cooperate naturally with the lower self, its human body system, wherein it is encased, for which BOTH parts are learning and experiencing, while the Soul is going along this path.

This is the journey into learning and growing, as each Soul will try again and again, to gain what it needs within the time that it is allotted on Earth, the current lifetime. And that time seems quickened, once the Soul reaches and starts to know, to intuitively feel, consciously and/or subconsciously, that it is closing in on its proper path for its given choices and talents.

Talents will start to emerge that will start to lead the Soul towards its destiny and the Soul will be gravitating to its choice, which we preset from here, in the Spirit world. But the Soul must journey to "it", the choice, for the opportunity to re-express itself.

Along that journey to re-express itself the Soul will desire to meet the need to "obtain it, *the choice* and make it all happen"! The Soul will meet again with obstacles that need to be overcome in order to succeed; desires that caused it trouble before, will arise again, such as the desire to drop out, to not complete the mission – the process of furthering its gift; the desire to walk away rather than overcome intermittent obstacles in life because the difficulties and demands are growing that must be dealt with in order to grow the talent, grow the gift; the Soul may miss its golden opportunity again, if it succumbs to its weaknesses, as in previous lifetimes and trials, attempts to fruition of goals, which met with the same frustrations and created for itself failure – more broken dreams. The chain of *disbelief* in oneself is then re-established, making it even harder to go further with the initial gift, which will insist upon its own time to be lived, as it was impressed upon the Soul in message form, from this side, Spirit, for that gift to re-emerge for use and fulfillment for *that particular* entity, on that particular journey into birth. Free will is all here.

Destiny is *the pull to the goal*. Destiny is *the message to continue on*. Destiny is *the determination to win*. Destiny is *the choice to further establish itself* within any given time frame, wherein the Soul will allow itself to gain knowledge of the gift. The gift waits to experience and grow into itself and seeks to establish itself with the core issue. Free will must be used to get us there, to fruition. **To "get it and get there, full expression of our gift" we must give ourselves permission to *believe*** in our talents and innate possibilities, coming to us through the experiences and accomplishments that our talents would allot us, if we would only first believe in ourselves and let ourselves have the experience. We must *step up* to have it so. We must *step up* to make it so. No one can give us what it takes. We must learn to FLY on our own accord and that is it…

Each Soul must learn its value and the strength to choose and stay the course with what it has chosen in its life. This is a strong life lesson that needs no opposition from within. However, opposition from within its own core **is the problem** from the onset and therefore, the Soul must *unlearn* all of its bad habits, some of which may have come through again to be expressed, in diminished fashion or with full strength, in its next body experience and have "influence" in disrupting the ability of the entity to obtain its goals and work at maximum life force capacity, using its energy wisely in what it creates.

Humanity has a history. Not all of us can establish the proper control when we get the next human experience opportunity, which comes through birth. It can be hit or miss! So much will depend on us. And sometimes there are circumstances that come into play, which will alter the course. It is up to the Soul to return to its course or path, and follow through to completion.

This goal is set from here, Spirit-side. In following that initial goal, it is up to each Soul, when it reaches the physical age of reasoning and then beyond that, the stage of personal power, wherein the entity can make things happen for itself, to act in its own best interests. The environment that surrounds the Soul includes family ties, which may sometimes be other than what we would desire for ourselves. This is not uncommon in any lifetime; we must *overcome much* to find and further create our destiny, waiting to grow and to be discovered.

We here, all of us that inspire from this so called "other side", can only hope that we have been of service and that we have guided well again, God's greatest creation, humanity. We will do all that we can but it is the free will of mankind that, in the end, must achieve. No amount of distribution of power from this side, Spirit, can make that happen on Earth. Each Soul must use its own power to achieve, to assess the given, everyday circumstances of its life unfolding, as it finds itself in that life. We cannot interfere with the final choices. We can only strongly impress our guidance, wherein it is necessary to aid the Soul at a critical juncture of its life.

Every day, the Soul must choose, and sometimes learning to choose, with discernment and in its own best interest, is very difficult. These lessons are hard on Earth, otherwise we would all quickly obtain completion and reach perfection in the human conveyance and never need so many returns to physicality to reach our goal of balance and then move on to live in the spiritual ethos, which is the world I dictate from.

We intersperse with each other's world on a daily basis but you cannot truly live here, on this side of Spirit, now, any more than I can fully live there, on Earth, with you. Do you know that this is a magnetic difference? Our polarities are reversed, yours and mine, and we cannot live in each other's worlds truly because of that fact.

Also, our density or refinements are different so we- cannot live in each other's worlds. Nor would it be wise to try to do so right at this stage of development. We will explain that later in another chapter or another book. For now, it is enough to know that our worlds are different but interlacing with each other on a regular basis and co- existing in the same space. Although it may seem that it is not possible, I tell you that it is just so and that is knowledge enough to gain in this text, at this time of writing.

We have discussed the issue of destined lovers, in previous chapters, but suffice it to say that *it is extremely important that we mate with those we love.*

If and when we mate for other reasons such as conventional reasons of sufficiency, everyday reasons of meager survival, then we will miss the golden opportunity that was to come to us through the experience of a true love. It is imperative to understand that each Soul has a destined lover. Let me say that again and be clear on this issue, as so many there, on Earth, have gotten it backwards. *Each Soul has in mind a true love to meet up with when it comes to the Earth plane.* That pick was made from here, in Spirit, prior to re-entry into the world of physicality, the Planet Earth.

Unfortunately, life happens on your side and sometimes it does not always go as planned. In the event that the destined lover has mistakenly married someone else, other than the one that was destined, then the remaining prospective mate is left feeling and looking for its other half and is truly in a position of loss. This is tragic. As the experience it had chosen to expand upon with its primary lover now will not occur. Then this entity must seek out another one to mate with.

Unfortunately, too many pick out someone that appears to be the "right one", the destined one, then will try to express expansion wherein no basis truly exists for this union. Appearances can be deceiving, often misleading a Soul into the arms of the wrong mate. How does this happen? Too easily so and too often we say.

If we could wish humanity one thing to understand about this involved subject, we would say the *heart is the best indicator* as to the whereabouts of the destined lover. If the feelings of the heart were not taught over and over to shut down the intuitive side, then the entity would learn to *trust what it feels.* This path would naturally come about if the Soul could learn to trust what it feels and simply follow that.

Instead, we see that the feelings and the tenderness of the heart, too often, there on Earth, get crushed and beaten down into submission to the mind, which is taught as and thought on Earth by so many to be the "wiser" part. We say that it is not wiser. The heart holds the message and needs to communicate with the operation system, the Higher-Self, so that the "link" with the already established pattern and choices set from the prior stratums here, Spirit- side, before the Soul took up the new life, *does not get broken.* Otherwise, the Soul will have difficulty connecting with its plan, and its life plan can get distorted. If and when this distortion occurs the Soul can get off the track of what it was supposed to experience and also not find its mate, because it does not even sense the right place or region of the country, its place and destiny point for expansion, let alone it's optimum partner.

The optimum partner is then left signaling for the coordinates and time frame where it gets to intersect with its chosen partner, but, once the partner has taken up with another, it does not find its target match-up. It then does not subconsciously pull its necessary data for field accuracy and acquisitioning of its mate. This data would be given to the Soul on the astral plane where it comes for re-charging when it sleeps, as its soul essence levies itself a little above its physical body while in rest. This process of re-charging spiritually the physical body occurs on a regular basis while the human is in sleep mode.

I realize that this sounds complicated, but life can sometimes get complicated because of the infusion of teaching that taught so harshly against the value of the heart and leaning too coolly towards the mind, saying the mind was smarter. Not so. The heart seed atoms are the cornerstones of all buildings that will remain eternal. Shrines of love will glow longer than the towers of glass in the vibrant cities that stretch their buildings to the sky as if to touch heaven. But these narrow lines in the air will never touch heaven. It is folly to think so.

Speaking spiritually - this misinterpretation is one of the many reasons for divorce. The Soul will in many cases, quickly find that it has not chosen the right partner and then cannot link or bind long term with its marital spouse. This is what causes the breakdown of so many marriages as the initial bonding process was not put into place; as the tie-in to begin with was misinterpreted and misguided; and was without a solid foundation from prior footings, spiritually established with a leaning towards intense sexual attraction.

This is also the reason for infidelity, as the Soul will still feel driven to the experience of love that it cannot achieve with its ready partner, if that partner is not in coordination with its mate. How does this get resolved then? In many cases, it ends in divorce, as people will attempt to find their right mate, elsewhere, beyond the existing marriage. This drive to find the right mate is a primal drive often accompanying heightened sexual desire.

So great is this gift!

A destined lover is the best gift that the Soul can ever obtain. How do you know if you have found that lover? You can answer that with your Soul. Only with your destined partner is that found to be a simple statement of fact. Only then can the face of the loved one be the end all and be all. When you have found the one, the need for this face, the sound of this voice, the desire and longing for this one, is a special calling, a special source of intense desire and pleasure. A pull to be with, one to the other, that is a grand thing to be experienced on a daily basis and so blessed, in so many simple ways. It is simple when you get it right. It is tragically complicated when you have gotten it wrong. It is better then, to wait for the lover that moves our hearts and takes us on the journey to love. Without that partner we may never find our core destiny; we may never find it and so all must strengthen their ability to discern what is the nature of their choices and wait for what is in the best interest of the Soul.

CHAPTER ELEVEN

REINCARNATION-THE TASK OF RECASTING SPIRIT

TO BEGIN WITH, of all the things that we have touched on so far in this book, this subject will be a fuller discussion than presented elsewhere, we believe. It is so often necessary to retrace our writings or to go back over what exists already in the library here, on this side of Spirit, which contains all that has been written for all of time in both the condensed and uncondensed fashion.

This process is not complicated; it is so easily done on this side, the Spirit-side, as we are not putting things on hard paper or hard discs of plastic or acetated materials. Use here is as a virtual, visual aid method using actual voices, if we desire to retrieve and review that "actual writer" as he or she went about the writing. We can even go back to the very moment the words hit the page and came into your reality there, on Earth, your very processes of mental perception and understanding of discourses as presented in those specific writings, whether those documents were cogent or immaterial.

It is also possible here to "*pull up the large screen*", to use the vernacular of your day, and review the overall status of the world in motion, as it existed on Earth, at any time. We can access the larger picture, an overview, or even pull up specific incidents or specific seconds of data, whenever or wherever that data was created and then study, review and learn from that data bank file. As I have said before, nothing that gets created ever gets destroyed. It still remains somewhere in the ethereal realm and we can and do access these things, *with purpose*, as needed, on a regular basis here, at Astara Central - Highlands, one of our spiritual world base centers, on this plane of consciousness.

Your time is not our time, as the calculated designation of time to us does not exist as it does in your world, by design. In your world it does exist, as designated by clocks, but in ours it doesn't, as time is a limitation that our ethos has no need of.

Clocks! This concept of "watching time go by" seems a necessity with all life forms that are destined to fulfill a limited period of existence in physicality. Emotionally driven, it is a necessary measurement tool for the entity as its life in the physical is only a short span, given the universal parallels of existence. Without getting too far afield, time is as necessary on your side as a rear window is necessary to perceive the changing seasons beyond it; a most generous analogy, but applicable for a meditation. Think about that!

All of these things are possible here, in Spirit, because nothing is ever truly discarded. In fact, the reverse holds true. If it was once created, it can either be recreated or it can stand as recorded in the history of the thing or personage, in full form, without modification or redress.

Therefore we are constantly reviewing, so much so that the individual who sits with us here gets a complete picture of how things are, how things were, whom they were before, what the circumstances were for them before, what they longed for and did with their lives and also what they did not do, and so forth and so on. Astara-Highlands Central, located above the Earth, is one of many centers that are set-up for this type of clearing process, aiding the progress of all souls through lengthy review and education. The Spirit world is not without its helpers and way stations designed specifically for aiding the betterment of humanity.

This is a lengthy process. It is a process that *all* Souls go through regardless of the level, or the age wisdom of the soul. All of this is accomplished with the Soul prior to the next recasting of their already existing Spirit essences, which are running in an accrued sense, lifetime to lifetime. Individualized information is stored as atomic seeds and only reactivated at the point of necessity, prior to re-entry into the physical womb.

Without reactivation of these atomic seeds, the soul cannot enter into human form again. This is the creative Spirit in operation for humanity. This has not changed since the beginning of life, the beginning of humanity. It is part of the overall operating system that is a core essential procedure and cannot be disturbed.

To disturb this existing process would change the nature of man. As we are not able *or permitted to* change that directive from the Creator, this is the method that stands, tried and true over the course of time through all known existences of humankind, on this planet or other planets, where we say, humankind *DOES exist* and so do other life forms of which we will talk about later.

"Ethos" in itself cannot be discussed without a differential scale of divisions and that is not something that is easily discussed. We wish to disperse that information at a future point. Herein, we are consistent with this stage, developing interest with the Earth plane souls that wish to root, study, and learn from the Masters that are now teaching through many leaders, such as Mrs. Lindsay.

It is not possible for us to change a thing that is of the past. Your film industry of Earth has written scripts to that effect, inferring the opposite of the truth. The truth is, that we cannot change the past, as the past is already written here, in Spirit, and recorded in the Akashic records. But the past need not be a predication or a prognosticated prologue to the future.

What the future becomes is up to humanity's further choices. By that we mean, we are *not locked into* repeating the same circumstances or we *need not err again* in the same area or manner as in previous lives.

Hopefully, examination here with each soul in attendance with our guides that do this as their main task over here, in Spirit, will lend insight and aid the soul in proceeding towards future wealth, wisdom, and prosperity of Spirit on their next journey into physicality on the Planet Earth. It is this "desire for the overall growth of spiritual quality" of the Soul that we try to strengthen before each entity receives its opportunity to approach the Earth plane again.

We will review all of these many lifetimes again and again, until the soul learns what behaviors were beneficial and what acts caused irreparable harm, although all acts can find forgiveness, eventually. That is the point of it. It just takes more lifetimes to make repairs and achieve the necessary karmic balance of actions. This is an ongoing aging of spirituality, which aids every soul as it is unfolding, growing, and naturally seeking the higher road of attainment over the course of many lifetimes or life tries, to reach maturity.

This point of equilibrium is lifetimes "in the balance or out of balance" whichever is the case. It is up to each soul to come again on your side, the Earth plane, and do its very best with its next body, mind, and re-cast Spirit.

This is the TASK OF RECASTING THE SPIRIT, recasting with greater wisdom installed in its planned outline, creating in the entity the potential desire to reach achievements that will increase the communal reference points *for all of the collective consciousness of humankind. And that is the greater goal, always, to seek to obtain!*

Upgrading of consciousness is created for all. What one creates can be shared with all, when the conditions are met for acquiring the information. This pool of information is little understood on your side, the Earth plane, although we would like to say here, within this chapter, that your science groups on Earth pull from this informative pool, this collective unconsciousness of knowledge and experiential data, on a regular basis, many times unknowingly, simply because it does exist. The fact that they do not know or believe of its existence does not stop the flow of the advancing information coming to them, information being drawn under the right circumstances.

What does this mean? It means that at a very minute level, we are all interacting with particles, atomic particles and other types of rarefied chemicals floating freely in the air and in the universe. As the combination of elements increases and as more of these unknown elementals are discovered, the use of the new combinations in science will continue to grow and make the future on Earth better and brighter. Humankind will be the beneficiary, as new products are developed from these newly combined elements and are able to be safely put to good use for the populace of the world.

Oftentimes the science groups of Earth, with what will appear to be randomly … "out there", stumbles upon what is, infact, set to be brought into discovery as "its time" *is set for discovery. When that time arrives, we send it over there to your plane, in thought form.* The souls that pick up the information are the ones that previously planned to do so from here; prior to their re-entry into a physical form, they have agreed to be ready, to have themselves installed, in place, befitting the necessary order to go ahead with the required format, bringing the discovery forward, bringing the product into actual, *physical completion*, which can be accomplished only on your side, only on the Earth plane.

We do not actually complete the invention or the thing here, Spirit-side. Our ethos will not support us to do so. But we know from prior eons of experience with your side, that your side translates the data and goes ahead with it. Always, *several people, several souls go out that can receive the "gift".* This assures that the world is not left without someone in place, on Earth, someone who will be advanced enough to bring the discovery to the world stage. This assures that the "gift" will come to the world within the time, in which we saw that it was appropriate, and safe to do so.

This would be considered a noble undertaking and those that accept do so, with a pledge of honor. They are honor bound to be ready for the "gift" and will inherently be subconsciously driven, almost from the beginning of their lives, to prepare themselves scientifically with the educational pursuit of excellence and skill in their given area of chosen discipline.

And most intelligent beings will credit their ancestral line for their personal gifts or credit their seemingly "lucky" "DNA." "Good genes" are often credited for the preponderance of genius, when it is actually a matter of reemergence of acumen and mental acuity previously acquired; we here, in Spirit, know that this person is building on an already established brain center of knowledge and ability, carried over from all previous lifetimes, all previous periods of achievement, in all prior lives. There is no loss; it is still within the Soul essences, only to be accessed from the operating system, the Higher- Self, when the aspirant wishes to do so.

In theory, to bring up many latent talents and areas of expertise established previously in prior lifetimes is possible, were the individual to be guided to this knowledge. However, each Soul derives the benefit of closure, from one lifetime to the other, in order that the Soul may be drawn to its new choices and not back to old choices for career and knowledge pursuit. This is a critical function, to move forward not backwards! This is why the information on previous lifetimes is not easily obtainable to the entity, as we do not want it filtering through the system, possibly damaging with interfering thoughts, the new operational guideline plan that is already in force in the new lifetime unfolding.

This is why most souls will have no ready memory of past lives. This is a deliberate closure, as past life recognition can devastate the entity, depending on the age of wisdom of the soul and depending on the gravity of what is picked up from former lives. (This is why regressive hypnosis is not for everyone and should only be done under very specific circumstances, with purpose, by highly qualified technicians.)

In this way, the soul can get on quickly with its business of current life choices and is not held back or hampered with rear view, derivative information, from the past lifetime files.

It is possible to access these records on your side through your Higher-Self; this request would go to your Higher- Self, directly, asking for assistance. In a coming chapter, we will discuss further on the matter of *the Higher- Self as a most valuable operation system.*

For the one that brings the "gift", the aptitude, and native ability of the scholar, ideally, would have already been demonstrated, the aspirant having already distinguished himself/herself in the area of scientific knowledge that relates to the consequential development under creation, showing the necessary quality of perseverance for the task. These critical criteria - would have already been demonstrated in prior lifetimes to even be considered for the task, as there would be many souls that would step up to qualify for the job and few that would be ready, given the degree and magnitude of the challenge.

The fact that the "new invention" or method of progression to the "new invention" is unknown to your world does not prohibit us in any way, *as we are always in advance of you*. After each lifetime, souls are routed to their groups for future development projects, tying in with all other like- minded Souls that have also studied in the same or related field of matter.

In this way also, the collective pool of information is refreshed, updated constantly, as there are Souls coming and going all the time, as lifetimes end and new lifetimes are beginning. This is how these things come about. It may read as one name on the patent on your side, on Planet Earth, but over here, in the Spirit world, we know the *whole story*. That is the truth of it. So mote it be.

As these things are viewed as difficult, these pioneers through invention have changed their worlds, through dedicated application of their great talents and unfettered determination. Against great odds and many times, great obstacles, these souls have stayed the course and served humanity well into the future, pushing the envelope of technological advancements and leading the Planet and its people through the widening pursuit of necessary progressions to achieve goals.

However, we are not always right about the projected use of the discovery! Sometimes, after discovery, these things get into the wrong hands quickly, when others come up with a dual *application for the discovery - an application that lends itself to destructiveness, which "application and usage" we did not plan, for the world to create. Unfortunately, weapons are created this way.*

It is the heart of man that must outgrow this need to be so destructive with his technologies and misconstrue what is sent over as the "gift" to be used for the advancement of the whole of humankind and promptly turns "the gift" into weapons of mass destruction, demoting the world into debasing, declining,

corruption! We again will talk about this "desire" before this book is finished, as it so needs to be understood at length and with proper information on a broader plane of understanding from here, Spirit.

This also explains why sometimes there is more than one scientist or inventor trying to patent almost the same invention at the same time. This is the *"gift" coming to fruition.* There is no other way to do this. As we must trust that the gift/invention/discovery - will be *delivered to the world,* we lend assurances by planting extra receivers (Souls) in the line of order, as a contingency to the plan, in the event one is necessary. Receipt of new inventions and new technological breakthroughs promotes the likelihood of a continued ascendancy for civilizations to build upon, creating more stability for the next generation, wherein further opportunity to establish advancement for themselves becomes highly probable, given the improved circumstances for humanity on the Earth plane. This is why inventions are so carefully watched over on this side and carefully released, in thought form, to your side.

Following along these same lines, it is not unusual to find a core group of the right people around the initial person that is to bring the "gift" to the forefront. Connectedness that had worked successfully before for a group of souls will many times manifest again in another lifetime with the same group connected to a new visionary product or development: ***A similar involvement experienced with other ventures will seem like "déjà vu" to some, but it is actually karmic ties at work.***

In this manner, the recasting of the Spirit is as a revolving door connecting the right Soul group, the right eras, the right dimension for the "gift/invention/discovery" to go forward. In so many ways we are simply meeting up again with each other, going in and out of each other's lives through these same venues.

This is commonplace in the Spirit, this knowledge of how things operate in the cosmic sense, as simple as you knowing that every morning the sun comes up and every night the moon shines over the blue planet, Earth. From observation and noted experience, you know that this is not a seasonal trend but a daily-established world pattern, which has existed through eons of time, recorded and stated as fact in your basic schoolbooks.

Which is not to say that all here in the Spirit are at the same frequency domain, but that at Astara Central - Highlands, above the Earth, there is an "unfolding" comprehension of the matters and wherewithal of the continuum and a wish to share our wisdom, truth, and knowledge with those souls that are ready now to pick us up, hear us, out of the chaos, out of a noisy existence.

Cosmic knowledge is not a dream. It is an inevitable reality that comes to the soul throughout the understanding of the continuum, which is a vast universe of considerations to be sure. Suffice it to say here, within this text, that people will do best when they have a cohesive reason to come together.

What could be better than meeting up again with those souls that one prevailed with in the past? Cooperation and a true feeling of fellowship have been at the baseline of many great partnerships of industrial minds and industries throughout history, the line of such personalities being too long to site here, histrionics being replete with so many terrific examples. And the world has needed each one of these leaders in order to receive the "gift". Therefore, it is providence when it goes as planned!

I have said earlier that things, inventions, plans, and methods for development from this side, sent over to your side for actual completion on the Earth plane, will not come forward until conditions are ripe. These "things" are simply held here, Spirit-side, until we are sure; as sure as we are able, that these devices created, *these new energies,* will be used to benefit mankind and not be used in a manner that will lead to planetary and universal destructiveness.

This is why we say it is so critical herein, within this teaching text, for people to realize where we are in the scheme of evolution. It is time for mankind to grow here, within this human timeframe. We are ready to lead on to the higher realms of consciousness, the higher realms of existence, when you are ready to follow and patiently delineate as you advance in study with us. We wait in anticipation, with hope, of such a great era of highly intelligent light beings, where we can help humanity in all matters of development, with the Earth coming fully to this stage of possible acquiescence. The dynamics of that acquiescence bear witness to the dynamics of a future we will talk of further on here, in this book.

So great is the destiny of man that we wish to end this chapter on recasting of the Spirit with congratulations to all that seek. Seeking for these higher realms and considerations leads the soul further in depth upon the journey of ascendancy of humankind. To wit, we are well upon that journey and we wish to say further that we are most positive with our thoughts to lead on. This can only be done through our continued due diligence with all of humanity. Humanity is in our care. We are entrusted with all of you there.

Know that this is the way of the higher realms. As you are there, on Earth, protecting and leading others to higher knowledge through discovery on your planet, we are doing the same here, in Spirit, from this realm.

This discussion leads us right back to the wisdom of God, the Creator. Know for tonight that He so loved the Planet Earth that He planned it for us all to find each other in the midst of our journeys. So large is His universe that we say it is beyond the consciousness of man at this level. It is so bright in the universe and we have only to continue on and to fill our lives daily with these higher teachings. And know that achieving receipt and conditioning from these higher teachings, when applied in our daily lives, with thoughts applied in sincerity and with reasonableness, in any lifetime, promotes the world and promotes the growth of our Soul throughout eternity. There is only but to continue then…so let us continue. ***He so loved the world that He thought of all of us in His great original plan, His great original genesis!***

CHAPTER TWELVE

"THE HIGHER- SELF - THE OVERSOUL IN ACTION"

TO BEGIN WITH, the Higher-Self *is* the Oversoul. The discussion in this chapter will deal with all aspects of the operating system, which is a subject that concerns all of humanity, as it prevails for all humankind. It is the essential method of guidance that was implanted from the start, in the creation of human forms. So great was the Creator, to imagine and then create such a fine "companion along the way" which would aid and assist mankind in the journey throughout lifetimes to maturity in spirituality. *So great is this most valuable of all systems to humanity.*

The bottom line here, on this discussion, is that the soul is never, ever, in any lifetime, *alone.* That it is always governed and assisted by its larger voice, the voice of its own internalized "master". This master contains so many necessary points of information that the entity does not even realize it is utilizing this system daily, in all of its thoughts, in all of its actions.

This system is a brain system, which is complicated and absolutely magnificent to describe. It will be a pleasure to explain the system here, in this chapter and I find it possibly the most incredible thing, this *Oversoul* system, which God created for man to use through man's many vistas of experience, while in a human body and beyond. Its operation and governance also continue on after each lifetime. It is in operation *beyond* the human body and we will explain that difference in operation, also, as we move along within this discourse.

The Higher - Self is a part of a universal community with all other Higher- Selves in service fully to humanity. It is possible for the Higher- Selves to communicate with each other and they will do that when necessary, usually in a subconscious way, without the entities being aware that this process is taking place, many times, while they are in a resting or sleeping mode. The human brain is more receptive to communication from the Spirit world when it is in the sleeping mode, as compared to its daytime functioning, which in so many ways constrains and confines, or, at least, is *interpreted* that way by so many humans.

The instrumentation of the operational system involved here, within this process, is sophisticated, to say the least. But considering that this *is* the universal standard for governance of humankind, *intended to work throughout all of human existence* on this planet and outer reaches beyond this world, it should be no surprise that it would be a terrific system; *as* mankind is God's most intelligent design and He is a genius in all things, creating as large in thought as any world would prove, simply by observing His end results, which He displays for us to observe, in motion, so many stars and planets revolving around us. How can we deny His existence? Why would we think it would be wise to do so? This is a point of meditation for mankind to ponder. And he would be so wise to ponder in that matter, sitting in peace and quiet, finding God from within.

Mankind is a learning, gathering, progressive design for expansion created by the Creator. Mankind is designed to continue learning through each life span. When a person returns to the Spirit-side his learning continues via a process of evaluation of the last life span. Likewise, pure academic studies will occur on this side, in the world of Spirit, and also other various methods of teaching, that our Spirit guides use to further instruct and bring illumination to the spiritual component, once it has left your side and begun its journey again, over here, after each lifetime.

This operational system, the Higher-Self, continues in force after life. Only upon returning to the Spirit-side here, after each lifetime, does it take the last, most recently compiled lifetime, from files containing the essence of what was gained from its life experiences, while on the Earth plane and while in the human body form. At that point, the system automatically runs a condensed version of the records for the soul and amends the data, adding this new information to its individualized Akashic record. In this way, all is updated and all goes forward, Akashic records and souls.

What comes about is a determination to further, by what was just achieved in the most recent life, the consideration of the goals for the *next* life experience! These reviews are never conducted alone. The soul always is surrounded with teachers for this time of *considerate* review. These things are never meant to shock or bring fear to the entity. While reviewing these details with the entity entrusted to us, we apply a "painkiller", for the lack of a better word, and a more dispassionate mood comes over the one under the light of investigation. Trial and error have taught us to be very careful in our approach, as we never seek to put a soul backwards, but always to move them forward. The gentle approach is our approach, never a punishing, damning, condemning voice of disapproval. The soul will learn to judge itself as it goes along throughout this process of review and counseling.

The brain system is a learning system. Humanity is only using a small part of its brain currently. We will explain in this chapter the reason for that and tell you about the possibility of expansion of the other areas of the brain, these areas that are not understood by the people of Earth.

Know that this information is to be used wisely. It is not recommended that anyone proceed with these documents in a *reckless fashion* or try to experiment with any information we impart here, in this book, as that is not highly desirable. Better that the soul who is seeking, wishing to learn, takes the time to study metaphysically first. The aspirant should study from hard texts, which are available, for obtaining the basic considerations that the student should learn. For a basic foundation in metaphysical, initial cosmic postulation, these understandings should precede in the mind of the aspirant, slowly but firmly permeating within itself, the knowledge being acquired, before ascending in acquisition, trying to acquire the more delicate and intrinsically difficult understandings, before the aspirant is properly prepared to receive this information.

By doing it in layered stages like this, it allows us to work with the souls on Earth in small steps and help them gain their basic instructions in a slow and methodical method. There is wisdom for these things beginning in this way. It is never our intention to rush these courses. It is so important to absorb the information slowly, so that the soul can properly integrate this data into its basic files and begin to use the data in its daily life, as it proceeds up the ladder of instruction with us here in Astara Central-Highlands, in the Spirit realm.

During the receipt of learning, a sorting begins to establish which of our aspirants are simply NOT ready for further studies. These will, of their own accord, drop out of metaphysical studies, at any given point as the studies become progressively more profound. This is the nature of the spiritual wisdom growth period. We do not look for every student to graduate to doctoral levels of thought, as we know that these understandings are not easy to ascertain and much is expected before one upgrades oneself with wisdom. We will explain more on this later.

However, nothing that was taken in by the soul will be disregarded. Even the completion of one understanding of how to gain wisdom, begins the necessary process of ascending beyond the basic living in the flesh. The soul will simply remember it. The Higher- Self will incorporate this knowledge that was gained, record it, and apply the knowledge gained wherever possible.

This is why we say that there is never a rush on our part. We do not think with limitation. We have waited eons for the souls to reach the progressive stage there on Earth. We say that it is more important to proceed with full awareness to the studies, a lesson at a time, than to force or rush these matters and accomplish no overall worth. What was studied will not find its way easily into the daily life unless integrated properly by the operating system. The operating system, the Higher – Self, is designed *to reject* many things if approached incorrectly. We will expand upon these things in this chapter, as it will prove to be interesting when considered in depth.

The Higher - Self is the most important function of the body system, yet is the one least understood by humankind on the Planet Earth at this time. Although what we are about to write here, within this text, will be disdained by many in the medical hallowed halls and Ivory towers of your world, we say that the following is fact: **The body of the human cannot function without the functioning of the Higher - Self.** When the Higher - Self leaves, breaking the Spiritual, connecting cord, the human body experiences death. The body will cease to exist as it would also not exist without its Spiritual component installed at the very beginning of conception. This Higher – Self system of governance is but an operational part of the spirituality at large.

Suffice it to say that mankind is *first and primarily* a Spiritual entity that *climbs* into a physical body that he or she will learn to manipulate through its ongoing operational system, which is known as the Higher - Self. This operational system is not static but is always growing and learning also; it is the intuitive speaking true to the everlasting.

This is an amazing data collection system designed, within its many stages of planned upgrades, to allow the entity to continue going forward in the entity's desire to grow and learn through its many applied life spans. It is universally the same in basic design and this design has not changed, in concepts, since the beginning of creation. Nor would there be a desire or need to do so, as we see it from here. We believe it to be an almost perfect, almost divine system, incredibly effective through recorded time.

As we can reference all previous time records, we can look at the entity's functioning gradations and begin tracking and grading the entity's basic maneuvering over centuries and over globes, this Earth being just one globe. We know this operating system, the Higher - Self, to be a grand vision of the Creator. You will learn that it is grand and broad as we go through this engaging chapter.

I have long awaited the opportunity to expand on this subject as I do not believe what I will say here has been documented before, at least not with the details that I intend to dictate to, Mrs. Lindsay. It is time for your side, the Planet Earth, to become *aware of this system*, as it is a magnificent blessing from the hand of God. It is time to recognize it and doing so will allow each person to communicate with his or her Higher- Self through daily practice of acknowledgement.

This is a primary, first lesson then: Simply acknowledge your Higher - Self each morning that you rise and you will open the door to a higher ability to communicate with it, the eminent composite of yourself. Also, to acknowledge your own Higher - Self, is to accept the reality that all other human beings possess a similar, individualized, Oversoul and therefore, *command basic respect and tolerance in our interaction with them in our daily lives.*

These two understandings, if and when humanity will come to believe it is so, will greatly change the face of the world. In the most literal sense, all things will change in accordance with this higher knowledge, the likes of which would be difficult to imagine here, upon this page, at this juncture, within the current Earth plane of consciousness. *Even to imagine* such splendor upon the Earth, which would seem unobtainable, is a most difficult thing to do, even in the minds of the most freethinking, high-minded Americans, wishing good will for all.

The Higher-Self can aid you throughout your life if you would ask it to do so. However, this is not a point of worship. It is but a point of acknowledgement. Active participation with it sets the stage for learning at a more receptive pace. Learning that the Oversoul and operating system does exist, puts us in the position of learning how best to use this newly found part of oneself, to the best benefit of oneself. We call into action our wisdom teacher to teach again, as we recognize we are not new to this experience of living in a human body. This is a great advantage and we will find life more delightful as our view is no longer so limited and depressing in its persisting theme of "one life, do or die" pressures. The need to be critical of others and ourselves in our daily lives will change and as we change, we will learn to become more cooperative with the

Spirit. We will learn to be more spontaneous! We will learn to be more open to the immediacy of our friends and loved ones that need us. We will make time for them under all circumstances with a better understanding *of how loving them* is the highest order of the day. The chores can wait a bit. Love first, when given the opportunity! "Love first and primarily". As we live in our human bodies, this will become a daily mantra for many entities.

The soul can use all of its attributes or very few. This is up to the entity. We will have many choices and the more that we choose to step up and expand upon our horizons, our abilities will grow to fit with those grander visions of ourselves and of our world, as it is and as we would have it change! As we learn to do this, we will rise in our attempts to achieve those larger, higher vistas of attainment, not just for ourselves, but also for everyone! This need to share with the world will become *stronger* as we move along, spiritually increasing our level of awareness.

Knowledge is not a flat line. Knowledge is always growing outwards and assuming many different shapes and sizes of containment as it ebbs and flows. Know this then, first and primarily: We can commune with our Higher - Selves. We may talk through to our Higher - Selves! Through meditation we can ask our Higher - Self to help us in a goal, to help us with a problem, to help us in understanding our current shortcomings, to help us do or achieve almost anything.

Also, finding oneself in danger, one can access the Higher - Self, observing the situation and receive guidance to an immediate plan of action to avoid oncoming serious harm. This system is designed to immediately assist upon direct request. It will respond if spoken to directly. It will attempt to communicate back immediately, almost instantaneously.

Know that it responds in a quick pace, it is not a delayed response; especially this would be so in the case of an emergency situation. Fear, however, may block the receipt of the answer. As the system is designed with a protocol and will not **answerback** with things that the soul cannot handle due to a large, overall, over-arching fear. Fear is a blocking agent. The system will guard against an excess of fear that could hurt or devastate or even kill the being it is standing over, watching, always watching in a loving fashion. This is a protective feature of the system; that it will NOT allow an overloading of FEAR to crush the current self. It will defer instead. By that we mean, it will stand aside and assist with a lesser response more appropriate to the situation in which the entity will withstand the occurrence of the event and not be frightened out of existence.

Also, it will not *interfere or overrule with a higher directive* of spirituality or otherwise, when the soul has made the choice to proceed with a decision that is detrimental. In other words, it will not protect, or OVER- RULE one, from experiencing the self-creation of harmful things or self-creation of new karma with others or other circumstances. Free will here is all!

This is where the free will of the individual comes into play. What the Higher - Self *will do* is overshadow, as much as possible, the entity that it is engaged with and *strongly send the message* to go away from what it is about to do, or say and try its best to *infer strongly* **the right action**, alerting through the mind, registering clearly within the consciousness of the individual, prior to the action about to take place. It will do its best to avoid allowing itself to fall into harm, **first!** It will flash images, pictures, words, replicate smells, or make any number of other sensory perception connections *to get the soul to pull back and remove itself from the detrimental action it is about to undertake. Immediacy is key here!* What comes *first* is the answerback from Higher - Self. *Pay attention to what comes through first.*

However, if the soul *chooses to ignore* what is sent from the higher governing system, which is set up to increase spirituality as a primary goal, it cannot stop the action of the person below it. This explains pre-karma in motion and free will in action. Attempts at increasing grace under specific conditions of extreme difficulty may succeed or fail. It is up to that particular soul to choose and the consequence of the action will come to bear upon itself. The whole system will receive spiritual merit or demerit with the choices made by activating the self that is living the day-to-day moments in the body. Building a strong willpower that promotes control over all of our emotions is key to the upward movement of humanity! Building character is like building stronger bones. This paves the way to endurance. And endurance paves the way to obtaining a "tenacious" attitude, which promotes positive choices and actions, which will see one through to reaching their goals!

The Higher - Self remains *objective* and is ready to extend love and compassion in the learning, in the experiences throughout life in the human body, regardless of the outcome. The Higher - Self is aware of the overall soul records of previous lifetimes and will realize that this is but one more lifetime to be integrated at the end of the span.

The Higher - Self is always in the position to take the longer view. Whereas, the current human brain will view only its immediate dilemma, overwhelming as it may be. In consideration of creation of previous lifetime negativity, it is a blessing that the soul *will not have conscious* recall of its bad actions, causing itself pain and suffering from this knowledge of events, as *it will have closure of memory,* from one lifetime to the next. Although conditions that the body may experience in the current life can *tie into previous* lifetimes and reappear in a new body, because these matters are unresolved from before, in some important way. We will discuss these considerations in a future chapter within this book.

After the current incarnation through the experience of death in the human body, the Higher - Self will assist again in all ongoing assimilations and evaluations of the most current lifetime and bring up for integration and evaluation the prior lifetime records for continued analysis, which purpose is to gain knowledge, grow, and prepare for the next physical lifetime. This is the main functioning of the Spiritual essence *out of* the physical body. It will continue and then, prior to the next physical journey into matter, it will resume its lessons here, in the Spirit and it will become a student again, preparing itself with gaining new information that is pertinent to the next go round in the body. This is what the Higher - Self does over here, in basic terms, how it lives on; we think that this is a good exchange.

We want all of you to know that life on the Spiritual- side, after death of the human body, is good, also. On Earth, there is so much fear of death and fear of non-existence beyond the body. We want to say *that the fear can stop,* if those that would read this book would believe what I am saying through Mrs. Lindsay. The Spirit does indeed live on and the journey to love is a continuing process; we must never give in to the pull of negativity that would lead us, for a minute, to think that we do not all have a purpose. The reverse holds true. That we are so purposeful, so very useful and we will continue on in these remaining chapters of this book to explain more about these wonderful things that we need to say herein this document, prepared with loving thought from us with Mrs. Lindsay as our agent.

It is our desire to continue on and say, regarding the subject of the human brain, expansion of capabilities for purposes of improved utilization and functionality will come. The expansion will come slowly and put forward here simply: There is no need to rush it. Over the centuries, mankind will simply increase his native abilities to learn and comprehend. As he does, his environment will also be changing around him and the concepts of the human body will also change. This is the way of future development. As all of that happens the brain areas in usage now will begin to come into expanded usage; at the necessary moment, joining into the existing lines of cellular structure with new lines, as it directs energy to carry the load. This will take centuries to come about as this is a major point of redeploying the use of the brain and its functioning is a major overhauling process that cannot be but a delicate event in operation.

May I say that the humans of the future will be better at so many things? For one thing the grasp of all things celestial will be upgraded and the ability to think deeply will also be improved. The normal needs of the day will have been greatly alleviated, as the terms of daily living that will coincide with these mind /brain changes will also be changed and greatly improved. It is, as it was before, a struggle to get there. This is why we take time in what we say here. Eons we wait for humankind to move up into these advanced stages of civilizations. Eons! Slow though it may seem, this is the way that has always proven to be successful, as we have seen this before in discovery matters.

Matters of brain telepathy will become commonplace as the human race will unfold with greater finite talents. These are talents that humanity is not yet ready to receive or put into action. Some will lead with these talents first; as this is the way we bring forth the consideration. It would be standard procedure that a small group would display these potentials or abilities to the world many years ahead of the entire world. Societies of people on the Earth will be coming to the discovery that this is available to all and that this is an application of raw science to which the brain can ascend. Now, the thought forms of the most advanced civilizations are barely aware enough to grasp the concepts, which are only in the infancy stage of realization of this talent and ability.

In your world, telepathy, in general terms of broad considerations, is not something that is viewed as possible by most. Accessibility, even if desired, is questionable; this we gather is the mindset of most. The same people would think it not possible in a real sense to acquire this skill, let alone - use it at will. The mindset is then locked into what it sees and regards as tangible. It is difficult then to get beyond those boundaries of limitation of thinking, to get into the frame of reference that allows for telepathy, which is a higher level of communication, completely understandable, but ahead of full understanding and discovery now, on your Earth plane of consciousness.

As stated before, we will not bring improvements to the Earth plane until the timing is as near perfect as possible, as we can see it from here. Remember that we are in advance of your planet from here, Spirit-side. We can see much of the future that might well come to the Earth plane *through astral projections* of a specific type. You cannot do that yet on the Earth plane. None would consider this ability now. No science group that is functioning on your Earth is in the processing towards that end now. Several groups study many other things and concerns of the future needs of your world. But we have not seen that they study hard, in an extensive or serious way, in this particular area of telepathy.

This subject will continue to suffer proper consideration because of its grouping within what is called the "mystic or magical realms", hocus pocus, or even black arts group, a mindset that is incorrect and static. Telepathy is no longer a subject that is to be discredited. Though it will take years, we think, for these attitudes of the masses to change. In the meantime, we will work with what we do have to work with and stay within those known principles that are accepted today, along with fact-finding compilations on the Earth plane.

Further, regarding the uses of the brain, we anticipate many gifts that will find a way into human experience. We will see the gift of new information *with mind levitation.* The ability to lift objects that far outweigh the human will become possible through spoken "word" to the object in order to command its motion and movement to where the human would direct it. The ability to kinetically link with the objects will be understood. *There is a new wave coming in co-relationship to this matter, a new law of gravity that is not yet known upon the Earth, but will become known at the time that these skills will* come to fruition.

The gift of rapid growth of food from fields will come. The secret to the ability to make food grow quickly is a mind device. This also will be a gift of the future to humanity. Water, most importantly, will be something that mankind will learn to *feel the presence of and* the talent to physically find water will be given to many that will come to possess this talent. These are but some of the gifts that humankind will experience the serious enfoldment of, coming in due time over centuries.

Majestic thought streams will come to many in the future and they will be led to a full-scale uplifting of their spiritual side, throwing off the coarse garments of hard-core physical hardness that has held humanity so rooted to the Earth. Humanity will then learn to become more ethereal although still remaining in its physical body; the physical body shifting into a redesign to accommodate the new gifts that it has received. These are but a few of the new, prescient gifts that will come to humanity.

The brain will become a more expansive tool. It will open wide in the future in order to reach for and broaden its future considerations. The race of humankind then will be similar to pioneers going into territories of existential living that is not daily living today. These things may sound as science fiction but sounding as unreal as they do, they will come to the Earth plane, as we see it today. Adaptation to the operational system, the Higher – Self, will also change to accommodate a metaphysical upgrading of all of humanity. As this occurs consciousness will become brighter than ever and the possibilities for sensational spiritual development will be remarkable, improving the state of mind of the people of Planet Earth. This time will be one that we will greatly appreciate as we the guardians sponsor the people of this great Planet Earth and long to see it enhanced in every sense.

So hopeful are we as we end this chapter on the magnificence of the human operational guidance system, the Higher – Self! It is our wish that those that read this treatise will learn to work with spirituality, which is live energy to be harnessed and used for the purpose of increasing abundance, joy and true contentment! Share always your blessings with other souls as you journey through lifetimes. Many happy returns! Go in peace!

CHAPTER THIRTEEN

GLOBAL WARMING-CLIMATIC CHANGES FOR EARTH

TO BEGIN WITH, significant changes on the surface of the Planet Earth have been building for centuries, working up to this time frame when we will have a shifting of existing conditions. Possibly, these changes cannot be avoided. However, taking action to circumvent *calamity coming* through climatic changes for Earth, would be best, all things considered.

Scientific studies are being conducted all over your planet and the conclusions are being shared on an international basis. Although these studies continue further on Earth, there is very little consensus on what to do about it! The idea of dramatic climatic changes for Earth, is a thought that can wait, for many!

Even the great minds of the people disciplined in the subjects that would govern these matters upon the Earth are afraid to speak of "it", the dramatic changing of existing conditions upon the Earth, as they realize the risk to credibility, the trust factor. They realize that the populace may not trust them if they speak openly of the impending doom. They might become listed as "full-mooners" or "alarmists" and may lose their very careers or jeopardize their positions in the world if they move too quickly to raise heated exchanges. So, many that could speak up now and lead a scientific strategy and planning team to be ready for these changes are not coming forward to assemble, with purpose, sponsorship or funding.

Instead, these things are being documented around your globe. Many watch these conditions on a daily basis. Many eyes watch, listen, and take scientific samples of specimens noting conditions of the samples collected, recording the climatic changes and rate of changes. But no one is sure of the overall consequences, let alone the proper correlation to the specific timing of these futuristic events. And as surety is something that the environment can never give, in absolute terms, many think it is easier to just *speculate to the public* and not *postulate the negatives that may befall the planet.*

Likewise, the political forces, the powers that be, all over the planet, do not want to deal with the impending futuristic issues raised by the facts of global warming and its deadly effects on the surface of the planet, or the existing living conditions that would be mitigated and the tremendous effects which all of this will have on the people who will survive. These survivors of the shifting will be the ones responsible for starting up again with life groups on the Earth within the new system, which system will then be designed, with emphasis on dealing with *mere survival* of the species - humankind!

Fortunately, enough of the scientific equipment, computer systems, and knowledge of all things technical, will have survived. Enough to utilize the higher skills that Earth has achieved thus far and these skills will be the difference between making it and *not making it* through these changes. The environment then will *not be the* environment that exists now. There will be so many alternating weather changes that I need to take the time here to explain first, *what exactly precipitates this entire unraveling.*

Fortunately, there will be the right minds in the scientific groups, enough of these people to immediately form their necessary teams and assemble at once with a *driving challenge to accommodate a new reality, wherein they must fight in a 24/7 fashion just to exist* and establish a new era in which humanity can begin again, but this time, very slowly, to restore itself.

This will take years and years of restorative talents applied and this we will talk about today, in this chapter.

The good news first…We will help those that survive through these devastating changes and required adjustments to your planet's climatic changes in surface environmental conditions, which changes we cannot see now as likely to be avoided. We have used our methods of astral projection to come to this determination. This system is a science method we have developed here, Spirit-side; one that is in advance of your known systems of applied sciences upon the Earth. We say, however, that mankind will come to the knowledge of these processes through ascendance. For the moment, let us continue to determine in this text, what we see is most likely to occur on Earth, given the circumstances that we believe causes the unraveling to pick up speed.

The unraveling is already in motion as we speak. What can be done now would have to be implemented almost at once, to delay the coming changes, which will pick up more momentum as pressure builds upon your Earth. These changes will not proceed in a flat, predictable rate of change, manner, or magnitude, but will grow much faster than predictable or *reasonably anticipated* by the scientific groups attending their notes and daily chartings of events.

The reasons for this are many but, suffice it to say here, the pressure grows and grows and weighs such on the prevailing conditions, which have been balanced and which now will fluctuate, unattended, and uninterrupted, *into imbalance.* As this imbalance grows upon the Earth, one condition puts pressure on another condition and then the gravity of the total circumstance is changed.

I am referring here to actual geophysical gravity, grates, plate tectonics, which are always shifting and moving, water temperatures which are always changing within a range and so forth and so on, with things connected to each other in the forces of nature.

This is important as to not be missed--that one thing ties directly to another, as this is a plan that has come into creation through the hand of God, *a genius designer,* and has been altered by mankind, due to his lack of "infinite understanding", which understanding only the Creator himself has. Sometimes, it is difficult to respect what He, the Creator, initially put into motion. We do not even know on our side or your side, or on other planets in other solar systems throughout the universe to **respect, the guiding** in **His genius and protective love, unconditional love of the universal ethos of all things. Genius! He is the ultimate genius! The ultimate "Giver" and "Lover"!**

It is difficult for mankind to know what things he is safe in changing and what is not safe to attempt to change. Eons we work to guide a slow progression into all areas that would leave the planet always within the balance guidelines required for maximum efficiency and efficacies restored and in place for future generations. Always, this is the challenge, but even more so, as the intelligent beings of Earth begin to come more into the realm of discovering their higher potentials. These times are now.

Humankind is reaching that stage of development when it is leaving its infancy in the world of science and about to go to its next stage in developing things and conditions for its world that are both necessary to accommodate the future requirements but also

95

more dangerous than in the past, because naturally occurring operational systems that exist now on the planet may be in the balance, at risk, if the groups that are making change upon the world *do not get it right.*

This is the basic problem; that things can get out of control and balance and be up for grabs. It is a difficult thing to get the environment in balance once it is severely out of balance. It *appears* that mankind is *not* destroying what God has created, but in fact, over years of misuse, he has done just that.

Ecosystems upon the Earth are being hurt as we speak and therein begins imbalance number one. Functions that were designed to work in conjunction with each other regarding barometric pressure, plate tectonic pressure, sea level pressures and air flow circulation patterns in conjunction with tidal activity, all of these ongoing natural functions are affected with dramatic misuse of manmade products introduced into the raw, native environment.

These conditions have been growing and picking up intensity upon your Earth for many years now as they are accelerating, pushing themselves into trouble that cannot be easily amended. As these pressures are building in the aggregate, and are not separate, distinctive stages of irresponsible actions but interrelated matters of occurrence building a resulting backlash to be experienced in future times.

This is step one, to stop abusing these things. We have to reestablish the natural order and balance to areas wherein these disturbances are now becoming of concern and obviously drawing attention from your scientific community on an international basis. Many eyes are now watching all of these ongoing conditions. But this is only half the story as the other half is that so few people are making the wiser decision to stop the continuing saga of disruption of natural balances.

If these things are allowed to continue, we will move into problem area number two which is *that the temperature of the planet itself will change* and move out of a range that is within its previous safety range, its previously established and recorded history of patterns. This is a problem because even slight differentials beyond what is known, acceptable data ranges, brings with it a devastating problem for the future, as it precipitates disruption with correlation to systems and functions, that then will also change in response to these rising temperatures.

Rising temperatures will cause rising levels of tides and much land disruption will occur over the years. Many more earthquakes will happen as the tectonic plates are shifted into new patterns. This will create disturbances in themselves from sealed off areas of the ocean floor not previously opened, causing new seizures, forcing up air gaps, creating environmental chaos which will result in high tides, flooding, earthquakes, and tidal waves the likes of which have not been experienced on the Planet Earth in eons.

Landmasses will then be affected as the changes will cause havoc, with some areas over the course of time being covered with water as the sea levels change, thus bringing the landmasses to a new level or sub level in relative terms of physical evaluation.

As these things come about, the populations of the world will panic and food shortages will come to the forefront, as the climate will be more difficult to predict. Areas that once produced food easily will not yield crops as before. The landmasses will not be able to do so, given the changes to the environment. They will be arid deserts and then there will be other areas, other landmasses that will be iced over in absolute contrast to the arid conditions. The planet will experience extremes and variances of weather conditions, which will disrupt the ordinary growing seasons for production of simple crops such as wheat and rice. The end result of these erratic conditions is that the planet, Earth, will not be able to feed the great numbers of hungry people that have amassed on the terrain.

This will lead to human behavior of all sorts that is a throwback to times of ancient, warlike conditions, tribal even, wherein people within areas that were previously organized, the people being orderly in conduct and law abiding, will find themselves in a new era of uncivilized, marauding groups of people, ruthlessly seeking the remaining stocks of food in order to maintain their meager survival. These days upon the Earth will be harsh for humankind.

Still, there is time to amend these growing, negative conditions. Many things could have been done now, but we do not see that about to happen as the prevailing thought is *to do nothing.* This is a real problem. Those that would speak, will not, because of the harsh treatment they fear they would experience for their vocal protestations; harsh treatment coming from the basic fear and intolerance of a world audience, which *does not want to listen.*

But we wish to say here that several noted scientists' surmise that many of the environmental problems stem from the use of the chemicals that are in prevalent use in your world. These chemicals are used in quantity applications, subjecting the Earth to pained, long-term results. Residues of these chemical products and by-products are now in your waterways and in your air and in re-circulating air currents worldwide. Meanwhile, these *facts seem to get lost in the consciousness* of the current societies, societies that have no idea of the gravity of these occurrences **and the results yet to be understood; the collective calamity yet to be reached and realized upon the Planet Earth**. Mother Nature would speak to you there upon the Earth, but we see that you are not listening!

Then there is the increase of ultraviolet radiation that is reaching the Earth due to a thinning of the protective ozone layer. We will call this problem area number three. As this UV penetrates through to the Earth, it will feed into the other conditions already reversing balance in slow, but steady levels, which will eventually disturb the balance of ecosystems in and of the Earth, with all conditions leaning towards growing degrees of imbalance. This problem then builds upon itself over the course of time.

Nuclear power plants upon the Earth will create huge problems in the future as we see that many nations will go back to build more of these systems, which we say is not good for the Earth. These systems are not good as this power has additional side effects to the Earth which are not being understood today, but will be understood in the future at the point that the polarity of the planet shifts. The consequences from these plants will cause explosive side effects around the globe, and many will die as a result of this power that moves beyond control of human hands. That will cause ignition of other land-stored weaponry that many nations have amassed underground; these stockpiles, the existence of which are not being revealed, one country to the other. But at this time coming, they will be a burden, as they will add fuel to the fires upon the Earth.

Weapons that once were created for defensive purposes, as in nation against nation, will then reap a staggering backlash upon the original nations that are holding the cache of weapons underground. As these areas are usually connected with territory that has people living in the same region, those in the locale of the region of the weapons will experience much devastation. These times, again, we wish to say, will be difficult.

Planned energy efficacies will become unplanned, as they roll forward in an unprecedented manner of destructive induction upon the Earth. Circulating air for breathing will become infected and impurities will cause immediate death for many.

Radioactive fall-out returning to the Earth's soils, after blasts to landmasses, will render the Earth unusable, unfit, and unstable for farming of any type for years. Food will become a major problem for the remaining humans that survive.

Here, on this side of Spirit, we are able to use a device called an *astral projection system*. We are able to take given scenarios that are in existence now and run them forward to create, in effect, test models of what is likely to be the future of whatever we are studying. This allows us to capture the future in progressive terms, view the outcome, and try to stabilize the current world against these projections that indicate severe changes into negative conditions for a planet and its peoples.

In the past we have been able to help civilizations avoid overall calamity. However, sometimes we are not able to do so. Such was the case of the great Atlantis! We wish to state here, within this broad text of considerations of the cosmos, that we do not wish to lose another advanced civilization to the hands of such calamity as was created by misuse of technological advancement on the great continent of Atlantis; a large continent that existed, which was located in the middle eastern countries; areas known today for their vast supplies of oil reserves, discovered and undiscovered areas.

In those times, Atlantis was considered the planet upon which all else revolved around it. Civilizations have since broadened their knowledge of the history involved, and know that this was not a planet but a continent, which even now, the remnants have not been located, as the proper location of Atlantis is still unknown to the world. We know that it is in the Middle Eastern basin of oil deposits. There is a geothermal reason for these oil deposits that do indeed, tie into Atlantis. We will talk about the great Atlantis at another point so as not to stray off of the subject of this chapter, interesting as it is, however, to speak again of Atlantis, what was and was lost!

Back to this chapter...this is a challenge for us as guardians. We will stand in the ready to affect the thoughts of the current people upon your planet now and to lead those in power to reconsider all of their actions that would lead to coming calamity which we have expressed in this chapter. However, Earth is particularly a great concern for us now, at the time of this writing, as so many are not listening and are simply "elsewhere" in their overall thoughts of global significance.

Communication systems by satellite are a great way to tell the world of its position on all matters. Your world is looped, one sector now to another. No longer does it take significant amounts of time for news of war and dissention to reach around the globe.

Now, it is within minutes that you can view nations in peril, nations at war, actively watching these things on your television screens while they occur. It should be dawning on many people that your world is running in the fast lane.

Many people have *not* gotten the message yet that you are responsible for what your leaders do. Participation is part of the freedom code. Your elected officials are only as good as *the good will and honorableness* of the societies that surround them and will hold them, feet first to the fire to uphold solid, productive, traditions that have been passed generation to generation.

There is no guarantee of freedom or democracy. The times of your world would be better if more would step up and participate in the processes that now exist, promoting freedom for all, around the globe. A sincere attitude of good intention here and now, would aid your world, if only the minds of the people could be more open and receive what we send over to you en masse, every day. These thoughts are a down pouring of our love and affections; strong affirmations for all that live on your planet. These are thoughts of inspiration to do all that is noble! From our side, the side of loving Spirit, we send you our best wishes and hope that you will proceed with the necessary changes to bring about good conditions regarding all things, all matters upon your Earth.

Even the thoughts of change that could stop the induction process towards negativity on the Earth; even this path could be changed, if only we could be heard by the many, instead of the few. However, it still takes the gift of a medium to go into pure translation of our words, such as recorded upon these pages. We are at least happy that we have this one golden opportunity here, within this text, to speak to the Planet Earth. This is a breakthrough for us, this side, the spirit-side, whenever we accomplish it, which we say is not often enough.

Meditation is one method to hear and receive us. Prayer is another and linking to us through guardianship is another way. Eventually, minds will learn to become responsive to what it is we send. This energy, once received, creates a connection that precedes a receipt of information.

Once the connection is made, the soul will become emancipated from its regular routine of drudgery of action and everyday attachments and will loosen its ties, which are strictly to the physical plane. Once this loosening begins, the soul learns to accelerate in spirituality and raise the energy in such a way to receive our thoughts, our powerful awakenings that we always send to help humankind.

This is the way of enlightenment. One step at a time, one day leading itself naturally into the next, always leading to an ascending path to soul fulfillment, the quality of which is lifted up and extended over the course of experience, one side connecting to the other side for growth of both.

Every day, we are beaming out messages to the Earth and trying to guide all souls to a higher level of existence wherein freedom and democracy will exist. We would wish that more would perceive what we send over. No matter, we will guide whether we are understood or not.

This is our message. It has not changed for us since the beginning of time: Your planet is but one that we guide; we *love all people and planets in God's universe, equally;* this is the pattern of love extended that began with the great Creator and continues through to this very moment; without this wave of protection, humankind would be at a loss to continue through to further ascendance through intelligence within its world plane, Earth.

In conclusion, I said that this global warming with events of climatic change *could be delayed,* but, as we write I do not see that humanity *will delay,* as it would take the strongest amount of determined will, applied across many fronts and agreement of cooperation one nation to the other; which is the true problem- lack of determination, cooperation and trust between the many nations upon the Earth. That the will of the Earth is not strong enough to let prevail, for the good will of all nations, with the best intentions of their people, as the main objective for all that is decided upon. It is easier to simply ignore these issues. Wars will continue for these same reasons; inability to cooperate and "fear mongering" proceeding agitation of wills to destroy each other.

The weather conditions will continue to build up a propensity that will lead to the shifting as described. What, you might ask me, Master Rama, would be the best thing to do here? How to stop these terrible things from coming to the Planet Earth? "Not easily done so", is my answer because the will of mankind is not strong enough here *at this point, to prevail in its best interest. Interest overall, which is indeed a matter of "survival".*

There is no consensus in agreement, by the world powers in place, for the prescription we have given in the details of this chapter, for a healing to coming conditions upon the Earth. Therefore, without agreement, there can be no overall solution to create a delay of these things, let alone firm plans enforceable to stop the destruction of this planet's resources; putting the environment at risk of creating the consequences of growing imbalances between natural systems and functions designed by the Creator to work in conjunction with each other for survival.

To put the environment first, all of its resources first and to the forefront - would take a magnitude of opinion followed up with raw action and the economies of all nations would have to shift their gears towards upholding the environmental conditions for stability and perseverance of purity of the planet's ecosystems, *before all else.* Can you see that happening, *now?* Given the current world status, I would love to say, "Yes" but I cannot. Yet, I would wish for all of you on the Earth plane that it could be so and these calamitous things, could be considered things that could be *prevented completely.*

CHAPTER FOURTEEN

FREEDOM'S CHALLENGE – STANDING ARMIES, MILITARY COMPLEXES

TO BEGIN WITH, as we write here with you, Astarian, your country with some of its allies is in another Middle Eastern war. The United States is waging war, a war that is to defeat the terrorists that exist in your world. This is a large and ongoing war, preceded by a war in the Afghanistan area of the Middle East.

As an adjunct to this position, prior wars were also waged in this area. Century after century this area of your world has been a hot bed of ongoing violence, open hatred, religious zealotry, tyranny of dictators and warlords, slavery of people, torture and all kinds of enforced methods of control over others in the region for the purpose of domination by cultures. These cultures hold extreme tenets at their core, and inflict much harm and destruction upon others, individually and in groups.

This has never been an area of your world where *freedom for the individual has* reigned; where freedom and respect for individual rights have been honored, protected by law and order foundations, solidly established. Nor do we see a system of community cooperation and end of social injustices coming to this area of Planet Earth, easily, let alone freedom and democracy for all. This area holds to the past with extremes in place today.

In this area of the world, to war in this way is the wish of too many of the people that, unfortunately, still believe in following their radical leaders who continue to teach lessons of intolerance, racial prejudices, and religious fanaticism. This does not permit acceptance of their neighboring factions; which their leaders have taught from the time they were very young children "to hate" and consider *these others* as enemies.

In a previous chapter, I mentioned "intolerance" as a leading challenge to humanity. In this region of the Middle East it is clear that intolerance is one of the chief harbingers of things to come, which will continue to cause peril in future days, as it has in the bad histrionics of the past, recorded on the page, war after war.

Even the oil cannot keep this region safe and secure. Not even with all the billions of dollars generated from the world, does this area gain its freedom from the past. Those that view it from the West do not yet understand what they are fighting. Freedom here is most difficult to obtain, as the people here, in this region, have a mindset that lets them be blinded again and again from seeing an obtainable, brighter future, replete with hopes and dreams of freedom and independence.

Instead, there exists a mindset that is but a continuation of an ugly humiliation, as in the past. Sadly, other than tyranny, many do not know any other way of life in this area of the world. It is a tough existence, a hard way of life that western, civilized peoples cannot even bear to watch as presented on their television sets, let alone handle the thoughts of having to live that way on a daily basis; *it is so upsetting to so many, bringing anguish and anxiety to the American Soul, which wants very much to win the war and move on quickly.*

As we have said in preceding pages of this book, the hatred that exists in the world attracts many karmic returns to the same region, wherein the hatred is then renewed and continued with fresh revenge fueling new engagements in war in that same region.

Most souls do not realize they have returned to pick up *where it was, they left off, killing and warring in a specific region* that has drawn them back *for karmic correction.* As these *ties* often involve families, it is fitting to note that the same immediate family members may reappear in new bodies, resuming family connections, as was the case in prior lifetimes, prior human existences, but, unfortunately, believing in the same fanaticisms!

Both points are to be remembered as we go through this chapter, as both points are important to the story of karma; *war and detachment, to future karma and future returns to war.* All of these things must be discerned in this chapter, as it needs to be explained here, within this treatise, in detail and with purpose.

There is much to say on this subject of warfare. It is a huge problem for humanity and has been so from the very start of the human race. The sins of war are many. To continue on with war *in this world, in this day and age* concerns us, your guardians and Spiritual teachers, greatly.

We are greatly concerned because, the need to control yourselves is paramount, as your weapons there, on Earth, grow more powerful, so quickly in devastating ways, across the globe.

This ability to kill en masse is growing in capability as we write, as the powers to be, with standing armies, are funded, with military complexes growing larger as well, around the globe. The world becomes more militant everyday with powers in place to war, one against the other.

Your greatest challenge to freedom then is <u>NOT TALKING OPENLY</u> and letting your military complexes do what they do best, defensive measures and wars of all sorts and everywhere, as solutions, for which we say, "They will never be solutions, as every war creates a new one."

And yet one would ask: Where is the diplomatic deluge of interest in settlement at the conference table? Why not direct talks on all *fronts regarding* all *matters, nation to nation? Where are the diplomatic corps? Why are so many* not even talking, *regarding these matters on Planet Earth?*

The United Nations chambers are not producing results that are needed for your world. Too many use this organization for a "cover", a front, to establish only what looks like good intentions, but many times it is not and it is merely a point of protestation for particular points of nationalism and exertion of political pressures on countries that would like to impose their will for commercial profit. This is why the organization is not nearly as strong as it needs to become, in order to be effective; we hope that the desire and willpower for change be forthcoming to that entire gathering. However, we will work with these leaders at their grouping place, at the United Nations headquarters, no matter the inundation of negative positions and purposes that are solely political nationalisms and not global proceedings towards world peace for all. But we remain, as always, *optimistic*!

If karma would be understood... a war ended is never ended, not forever. Much must be settled that occurred within the war structure regarding the entire matter. Perplexing as this may sound, this is not a simple matter of attraction, but a matter of one thing balancing out another. This is really about cause and effect.

You should always remember: these things go hand in hand…cause and effect! Watch what it is that you create.

Call a thing by its exact name and know it. Create it not in thought or deed unless it is required or desired. Pay attention to watch what you do and know that all of it is important, in specifics and in general terms.

That is the larger message: <u>one thing is connected to the other</u>. So, it is always. Know that you must untangle what you have tangled. Although you cannot move backwards in the physical, the remnants of what you have created will follow you in form and circumstances until they are completely offsetting each other with balance and attunement.

I realize that this metaphysical lesson is difficult, but to understand war one must understand peace and know that the two are exactly related to each other in opposition, yet must be understood, with one standing next to the other for proper observation. This is a point of meditation. If you can learn to view them this way, you will start to unravel what it is that keeps you from what you desire most - war or peace?

Now we see the Earth at the crossroads with these two things - its standing armies and the military complexes that support these armies, fully funded, fully mobile. Must we remind you here, again, something so obvious? That your Planet Earth is a sphere and is in fact moving in an orderly solar system? It is but one Planet that is in a larger solar system, the full dynamics of which your scientific societies have not explored, fully, end to end.

There are others, from other solar systems, which have explored beyond your blue Planet. They are not for discussion in this book; perhaps, at another point in another book, if there is a purpose and need to go into those things, then we will write at that specific juncture. But, for now, we have our work cut out for us with these crucial matters. This discourse is about Planet Earth.

Warfare is NOT the answer. I am repeating that again…WARFARE IS NOT THE ANSWER! To solve everything with a new war is absolutely not in the best interest of the humankind that live on Planet Earth. And the sphere itself is not made better within the occasion of these things.

Also, the fact that the Planet now has reached the point of open terrorist activities, which are serious violations of peace efforts, the ante has been upped. The game plan has moved to a new level. The citizens of the United States have abdicated authority to the throne, so to speak.

Your constitution was never written to be in the hands of the few. It was designed to remain in the hands of the many. It was designed with a firm idea of checks and balances that would produce a proper balance between your three branches of government.

The presidential power to make war has been increased since your country experienced the tragedy of September 11th! New York City will never be the same, as it will always remind the world of what has been lost. It will always be the slaughter of innocence, on that day in September, which awakened a sleeping giant, a giant prepared to strike back.

It was on that day that the skies of New York City were filled with smoke. On that day many people in two tall buildings called the "Twin Towers" met quickly with an astonishing death. As the world watched on its television sets, as passenger planes were diverted, one to Washington, DC to hit also your Defense Building, the Pentagon, and then the other plane was so bravely taken over from onboard terrorists by those brave souls, that took down their aircraft into a field in Pennsylvania in order to avoid a more serious occasion of death for others, if the fully loaded passenger plane had reached its target. These events have changed the world.

The perception of peace is now a stalwart perception. The giant is now clawing its way out of a larger morass. And so, it is no over statement to say it is a race against time to prevent future casualties of war upon your Planet, as the United States is now leading itself into further troubled waters.

Though the United States would believe that it belongs in the Middle East, we say that this is not wise. Extrication from the area as quickly as possible would be wiser for the people of Iraq must now fight for their freedom. Teach them the skills and then they must reach for their own floor of democracy. The United States can only protect them for a short while longer, then it is up to this country to let its people fight to maintain its own law and order system, hopefully, its own democratic rule. There is no peace that freedom knows like blood upon the rose!

Annihilation of other countries rising to give the United States trouble is not a proper solution for future planning either. This is a time to be cautious with the power we held and to yield to a diplomatic table as much as possible.

War, and detachment from it, is part of the necessary process for ending attraction to future war, wherein new karma is created. To learn that you must not create war is to understand that peace is not given proper sway, proper consideration.

This is a powerful attraction, war, as revenge, is at the heart of so many. War waits to be rekindled as hatred continues to build throughout humanity, throughout history, one group alienating the other. This is especially so in the Middle Eastern region, wherein these wars have been going on for century after century, and the area has not known a solid peace for any length of time.

Detachment must be gained. This is done with daily application. You must learn to forgive immediately and not hold in your emotions. You can have your emotions and express them, but within civil tones and civil exercises. If you can learn to forgive instantly, then revenge would not come in and steal from you by creating new plots in the future, wherein you create new serious circumstances, where you hurt yourselves through hurting others, in the course of getting your revenge.

Violence is not an acceptable response. You must train yourselves to believe in the power of love and tolerance and immediately learn to accept all and under all circumstances, circumvent acts of violence. If you want to be more peaceful, you must teach yourselves first, how to come about peacefulness and how to conduct peacefulness worldwide, in your interactions with others. They will follow you to peacefulness then and not war. You can lead them to either! The choice is yours. You can conduct yourselves in either manner.

Too many today create havoc and unhappiness within their mindset. Too many worry themselves into anxiety and do not even enjoy the day they are living because they are either thinking in the past or thinking ahead in the future. In the meantime, the joy and rewards of living in the present moment and appreciating exactly what that is, gets missed. The pattern is to repeat through the mind(s) what cannot change the past, or focus intensely on the future, which is not here yet to effect in any way. Each human being must learn the value of the moment, live and appreciate that moment and stay in that richness of existence.

Discipline is at the center of life. To discipline the mind is to create a mind that is preparing to achieve whatever it wishes, because it will create a balanced world in and of itself.

Happiness is derived from this inner balance. The soul is not lost on its journey through this life then and will not need to resort to taking drugs, abusing alcohol, using cigarettes addictively, or finding anything else suitable, for creating obsessive usage of that thing, to your undoing, overall. Escape will not be attractive. The aspirant soul will naturally look to maintain balance, as he or she learns that this is the only way to work well and live well in the human body.

This way of living will create a happy family environment and the children that are raised in the household will also prosper, as their parents live well and love well, having found a lasting peacefulness.

The acquisitioning of all things will then be a secondary consideration, as the people and the relationships of love in the household, will take precedent over all else. After that, this need to give and achieve balance will flow over into the community, the church and the neighborhood and this is how a structured society, linked to its neighbors, is brought about. This is not an abstraction, but something that you must learn to do, something that must be taught, parents to their children and then children to their own families when they grow up, experienced on a daily basis, one day at a time on Planet Earth.

Worship of God is also a key to finding peacefulness. It is not the choice of church that one should deliberate about, but the choice to love God and see God in all the other humans on the Earth. This is good karma in action. Set those thoughts upon the world, and the world will change drastically. Improvements will follow leading the way to sanity and healing of Spirit, mind, and physical body. This could be.

It is not your standing armies, military complexes and weapons systems that will save you on Planet Earth. It is in understanding that you do not need magnificent defensive measures against each other in order to protect yourselves. You must learn to build bridges and contact each other in the spirit of true humanity, establishing a world system that fosters change in a positive direction.

Your weapons systems create more wars in order to use what you have created. Billions and billions of dollars wasted in order to "build protection" through devices that would kill whoever opposes you. It is your own mindset that needs to change, your own belief system that is lacking.

With every new weapon you create and put in your hands, you are reestablishing the link to the belief that created it. **The *belief that war must always be* and that weapons will always be necessary**; the belief that wars must be considered a thing that will always exist; the belief that to allow thinking otherwise would be considered a lack of responsibility, in a world that holds itself accountable for its own defense; a defense that continues to grow, one generation to the next, raised up with the same belief in the absolute necessity of war and remaining militarily ready for these future engagements.

It is your belief systems that must change. Or, humanity will continue to create for itself new battles and revenge will bring you back to revisit these issues, over and over again. Detachment is the only way out. Consider that there is the other thing called "peace" to postulate and then peace can take sway and consideration.

Why must it always be that war is considered a thing that always will exist and "Peace" is a thing always to be IMAGINED? Why, ask yourselves why? This is, also, a point of meditation.

These Karmic connections are often returning to old fears, fears that you have not learned to let go of. You have fear when you do not understand. There is much that would block you while in the human body and nothing is quite so difficult to overcome as basic fear…fear of a person, a place, a thing, *even a feeling*.

We must discuss fear here, as it is the appropriate ending to this chapter. Only in this case, it is national fear. Why build standing armies and military complexes, anyhow? Fear…fear of your neighbors, fear of the possibility that some other country may interfere with you and even destroy you with their weapons. Therefore, you must have your weapons to fight back. The race for building weapons continues, on and on through time in memoriam, time immortal and many will die as in the past, attached to their fears.

Fear will keep you all in chains. Fear will keep you building stockpiles of weapons into the ground and maybe even, fear will lead you one day into a larger war that will cause severe peril, the likes of which you have not seen yet on this Planet Earth.

Fear, is a stumbling block. Reduce all fear and release your thoughts to the opposite of fear…trust. Always view the opposite of what it is that you desire, when doing battle with a thing. View the thing that holds you back from your achievement right alongside of what it is that you would have. Then, rest your mind on what it is that you truly want? Think about this hard as in a deep meditation. Then you will start to unlock the truth of these matters.

Standing armies and militaries complexes are, indeed, freedom's greatest challenge. In this day and age, you cannot get to world peace without addressing the larger issues of trust. These are much larger issues. Why is trust so difficult? What is the opposite of trust…suspicion? Slavery of thought is at the basis of all things; century after century, the human soul returns to human form to deal with itself. Fear will hobble the soul again, unless you can learn to grow beyond your fears.

In an earlier chapter I discussed fear, go back and reread, here, take a pause in this book now and please reread what I shared with all of you, about the basis of fear and why it holds you captive, keeping you as prisoners in your daily lives, wherein, you are not able to move beyond it, accomplishing what you would wish to do and achieve in your world. Fear is primal and must be understand as such; otherwise, you cannot override it with your wisdom minds.

Know a thing and call it what it is. Diagnose yourselves immediately, approaching yourselves from the perspective of objectivity, viewing yourselves wherein you find your pathos, your ailments, your reoccurring areas of dis-ease and discontent within yourselves. This is a method of teaching, that you must learn to appreciate through practice as you live and use as a point of due deference, within your comings and goings, within your relationships with others in your very involved and complicated lives.

You can complicate, or un-complicate yourselves. This is your choice. Choose wisely then! In watching what it is that you choose daily, you begin to call that thing by its right name as you are paying more attention to what it is exactly. You will then see the larger picture, which may give you a clue to solving this puzzle…life, with you in it, life that is both, apparent and unapparent. You are many things, daily!

This is a point to understand: mastership of self is not easy! Otherwise, why would you have to revisit the Earth and start again? Why? It is a big help to know that we are older

Spirits then, as opposed to just starting out. Think of it. Which is easier, knowing that you are in first grade or finding that you are really in high school?

See what I mean…. Give yourselves credit where credit is due. ***Acknowledging, when you succeed is imperative, applauding yourselves as you go.*** This is a time to celebrate. Celebrate, when you are called to a larger truth. Choose the path of enlightenment and discovery, putting your hearts into furthering this great Planet Earth, helping all others that are upon the Earth plane, simultaneously with you. It is a shared journey. Enjoy it and the growth in the Spirit!

Practice trust. Trust and love, these two things will truly set you free! From the depth of your souls you need to trust and you need to love and you need to do both at all times. ***There is no larger mission for humanity than TRUST AND LOVE! So mote it be.***

CHAPTER FIFTEEN

REJUVENATION OF SPIRIT THROUGH RECONCILIATION

TO BEGIN WITH, reconciliatory expression immediately after severely being injured by another in thought, word, or deed, is a very difficult thing to do. It is a *state of heart* that needs to be established within the psyche. This should be a habitual thing to encourage ourselves to do - to teach oneself to immediately undo any wrong that it has created around itself. Learning to do this one thing, in any lifetime, sets the stage for a more morally, easier accommodating road to follow in **future lifetimes, presenting the soul with a way to immediately reduce karma, setting the stage for subsequent rebalancing of *cause to action.***

We are then training ourselves to rejuvenate our Spirits through right action. We are then lifting all of humanity and ourselves higher. As we embark upon the role of leader and teacher, to all those who are observing us within our immediate circles of friends, family, business associates, and communities of neighbors, we are teaching them the path to attainment; the path to peace and harmony, side by side.

Even strangers, perhaps being unable to explain the feeling, will observe a basic elemental difference, a difference in the field radiation moving forth from the dynamics of a Spirit, *a personage*, which is constantly in the process of rejuvenating, converting all things to a higher plane of balance. A difference will be picked up in perceived feeling and/or presence, projected out from the individualized Spirit of such an individual, whether being viewed or heard from afar, even just speaking, such as in a telephone conversation, the personage will register their innate print. The written word also carries the "interior trademark" or *exclusive* imprint of the person writing.

The Spirit prevails through all of its inherent properties for personal expression. There is no way to stop the revelation of our Spirits, no way, whatsoever. And we should encourage ourselves in all matters to be exactly who we are, as this is a privileged, shared event, one soul to the other. Quickly, we can learn to appreciate what is essentially pure from the onset of discovery of others and ourselves.

It is tempting to go through life and make no stand for our individual thoughts. But this is not the way. The polemic groups should have leaders, but the people must fend for themselves in a democratic society. There must never come to pass the loss of the rights and freedoms: the thoughts and expressions of individuals, as long as these things are within the scope of jurisprudence, then the law-abiding need to always be who they are and *say whatsoever it is deemed necessary for full expression. This is the way of spiritual scholarship achieving in action.*

Accommodating a different point of view is essential in accepting other societies and other nationalisms in the world. Your countrymen, in the United States of America, need to allow for the voices of the average American to be heard and respected. Always, there should exist, accommodation and consideration, in whatever laws are passed through new legislation, whether in Washington DC, or state by state.

New legislation should always be for the good of the country and then we will know that right action is at the core. When *right action is at the core, even our mistakes, of which we say there will always be mistakes, we can admit to. Upon finding these errors, we must have the courage to say we have erred and then, upon acknowledgement, reach for the necessary accommodation of change. That change should extend aisle-to-aisle. Congress and Senate, hand-to- hand, neighbor reaching out for neighbor! So, this thing grows. Peace and harmony are achieved in this way.*

What do I mean when I say, "basic difference in the radiating field of a person?" There is an immediate feeling that the soul projects outwardly to others as it comes into contact with the field of the other entities. Each time that we meet others, we embrace each other's aura and the magnetic energy field extended from that aura. This is a matter of natural consequence and we will feel these souls at once, but may not readily know that we do this with each other all the time. We may not see these fields, which are as shimmering, iridescent rainbow effects in various shapes and proportions, but they do, in fact, exist around each individual that is alive and can be felt impinging, through sensory perception, as they vibrate, in wavelengths, one to the other upon contact.

Those that mesh with us *will come to us to embrace us more than others because that chemical attraction and electromagnetic field will attract. Those that we are repelled by will not come to us, as we will not have a basic attraction to them, as the fields are not consequentially enhancing each other.*

What I mean by "enhancement" here is, essential matching correspondences. This is individual and each person develops character in each lifetime and builds upon the basic nature that has been continually growing within the soul essence through each lifetime and thereafter, as even on this side, the Spirit-side, it continues to grow. This is the *nature of this matter of this we are sure.*

Now then, if we can learn to grow and let go of our mistakes as we find them in others and ourselves, we are quickly readying the road for a mindset that is able to handle all of the obstacles that life will present. And it is the nature of life to present obstacles, as there is no perfection in truth. Perfection *is* a process and projection that is constantly growing! We have said this in previous chapters herein: "all things, whether we are aware of it or not, are in progression and that progression continues whether we acknowledge it or understand it." These processes will continue to make their progression, as is the set course for these developments to do so, as the "word" has been set in motion to lead these matters to do so.

And this is the rule, generally speaking, of all things not human in the universe of cause and *action, in the universal scheme of things, and on your Planet Earth, the blue planet.*

We see Earth here as a beautiful blue planet and wish that all would accommodate each other and through all things learn the art of combining and compromising values, harmonizing with each other. As we learn the art of giving, a little more of ourselves here and there, we are letting others around ourselves join with us in their efforts, which may require the need of accommodation, as their essences and efforts may be different. **But being different than ourselves does not excuse us from *the matter of caring for others and seeing to their welfare.***

Even worldwide, this is the overall challenge, as all of you there are on the same planet and in charge of it. You are all in charge of the Nature of the planet and the consequences for its development or lack of development.

Especially this is so, now, as the development of humanity is being challenged and moving into scientific areas of expansion and exhilarating science gifts that will open the doors for space travel, even to new worlds, to be established on other planets, once the process of how this is accomplished is understood by your higher scientific groups.

I want to return here to a further discussion upon the loss of love mates, as it is so difficult for so many in the human form to accept. A wider understanding will expand consciousness on these issues and hopefully, a deeper healing and spiritual rejuvenation can begin again, herein:

The lamenting for our "Loved Ones" is needless and we must accept that they are not dead. The lamenting is natural but best released upon contact. The contact point of release comes to us through the acceptance of the life lesson and principle of reunion. Compensation factors will draw souls together again where any love connection was seriously set in motion. *This is called the law of abiding compensation.*

That love mates will meet again is as natural to portend, as with promotion. Consequentially, in the cause of the future reunion, follows as naturally as the conclusion of the matters of today's business flows into tomorrow's business; as the material manifestations in our daily lives run in the aggregate tying directly into energies that have made the basis for this reality and prior realities. This is cosmic law. What goes forward can run backwards in connectedness. This is a point for meditation, one of many. The people, places, and even location of our homes are in direct correlation to what has been set in motion. Make no mistake about it, these things are not unplanned, but will follow the natural order of the thing called - love connections. This is real, tangible energy, energy to build with and energy to destroy the things built within the realm of management, or lack of management, of our self-created "empires", self-created domains, which stretch the boundaries of our existences across all planes.

Containment or unrestricted destiny is our choice. Expression within opportunity is our choice. Our choices are out there, every day, every hour, and every moment. What we think is creating and or destroying. It is important to recognize that this is **live energy.** Use it well and promote reconciliation where required, across the board, in all matters that *represent our very existence, our modularity in our daily lives.*

I wish to review, to tie in, that in previous chapters I said that the soul had a general outline and that that outline continues in force until the last moment of existence for that soul within that particular incarnation. There is no way to change the soul programming, as the program is registered in the operating system of the Higher - Self which is a part of the brain functioning, ethereal software- like installation that takes place before the seed atoms join the fertilized egg at the start of conception of the human form. Intelligence and soul transfer happen immediately upon implantation. It is a design that has served humanity well. This in no way inhibits free will, as the program is but a general outline and the soul must choose and make choices for itself as it develops again in human form.

When our plan, the general outline, is interrupted due to circumstances that have taken us off course, that delineation forces a change of direction in our lives. But, the original guiding plan is still in motion and will seize the opportunity to propose a redirection, but back onto the original course which will again, promote and propel us into the line of fire; the line of people we were intended to meet up with and settle our mitigating circumstances with, before our current lives have ended.

We have said in the chapter on the Higher - Self and the operating system, that this plan is a functioning of that system. Choices to deal with pertinent, particular relationship debt are made and taken on as an assignment prior to the current lifetime. This is the nature of the karmic connection of which we say there is good action to promote and good action that must be promoted to resolve karmic problems - the residue that needs to be remedied, healed and reduced into the rejuvenation of our souls.

Fear must be overcome in order to work on our issues. Resistance to working on our issues with each other is proof positive, an example of existing karma that refuses to budge and finds difficulty moving along, or being processed.

The choice of rejuvenation of Spirit through reconciliation, when brought into being, will bring us to the resolution of our conflicts. However, there are many ingredients in this recipe.

It is not only the ingredient of "immediacy" that promotes resolution. It is not only the ingredient of physical proximities. There is much more that must go into the mix of the individuals in - love connections. These matters can be delicate and mind-boggling.

Sometimes, we find that the souls are not ready! Not ready again to solve any built-up conflict. They are still not ripe for the process of healing and resolution, or finding a bridge to a new beginning with each other.

If this is not solved in the current lifetime challenge, then these matters, in the case of lovers, move, most assuredly, to a future lifetime. These two souls will be drawn again to each other until the opportunity to meet and review the conflict presents itself. The tension will reappear, and even though the couple may find themselves intrinsically and inexplicably attracted to each other, there will be an undeniable push-pull, this thing that tugs at the couple under the surface of words and actions, in their current relationships with each other. This thing that tugs at them is their previous karmic connection.

Irrespective of the current lifetime, the couple will either move into a sexual position with each other or not so, depending on the intensity of the moment. Sexual contact only promotes the feeling of connectedness. It does NOT, repeat, does NOT promote the healing, necessarily. It can heal, but may not heal, if the underlying conditioning of the two people involved is not motivated at the level of harmonizing with each other.

It is as if they meet again to love and embrace and just as quickly disappoint each other and break up with disillusionment, even then, not knowing what has happened. What has happened is that they have unmistakably moved into a previous karmic tie and have again failed in all attempts to mate with success. Success here is being defined as some personal and notable level of attainment of a significant state of their being that would represent happiness in mind, body, and/or Spirit.

This is why we say it is so imperative to *wait for a love match* as each soul has indeed intended to mate with a specific partner. As difficult as this may be to fathom, it goes like this…a partner is also always looking for its proper mate. These things are chosen from this side, the side of Spirit, prior to any new life. Progress, ideal progress then, is to meet the one that is chosen from here for re- involvement and reinvestment. But, to make that happen, many things have to go right on your side, the Earth plane, and this is where the problems come in, as sometimes the adjustments necessary in finding the right mate, the exact one, are serious adjustments.

Sometimes, the mate ends up with someone else that he/she simply felt a strong *connection* with. This intensity can be deceiving. Unless the entity has studied about previous lifetimes and how this process works in specific, this feeling is not properly put into perspective. The soul may well move ahead with the one that it has found and that connection is real, usually from the past, but not necessarily the one that was designated for this particular life venue.

This *mistranslation of feeling* sets up a scenario where "the couple", the true love mates, never meet, never marry and never get to fulfill what it was that they planned to achieve, as in the general outline from the other side, before this current life span. The point and potential of ideal destiny then is lost, *but only lost to this one lifetime*. It is then passed to another lifetime for re-discovery, and this is how it goes.

But, when love mates do get together, as planned in the outline, bliss is assuredly felt. So also, are the deep feelings of loss at the point of separation from the love mate due to death of the partner! Then, the consideration of the matter of the remaining mate left on the Earth plane after the death of its true love is significant. You may ask, "Is there another true love to come and take the place of the one that left?" This is another point of impact, another point of study. The answer is sometimes "yes", but not always. Let us discuss this, then, as follows....

The soul that has lost the true love mate will have the choice to finish up with all other lessons, life lessons that it has not yet finished.

Always, there will be secondary lessons to pick up with and get into life again with, full speed ahead on all fronts. The time for healing will be a matter for that soul. The sooner the soul accepts that the mate has moved on to a higher plane, the sooner the remaining mate will benefit and make good use of the remaining lifespan.

What the soul chooses to do with that time left is up to itself, as most of the initial goals have probably, or most likely, been met through the course of the experience of loving and living with the true love.

Loving and living with a true mate is the most ideal choice for a husband and wife consideration. There is no greater joy than the joy of traveling through life with a true love. The lessons that are to be learned will be done so easily and joyfully with the knowledge of a true love, to come home to and embrace at the end of each day. There is no joy as great as that joy. No sexual happiness to match the contentment of sensuality with a true love. It takes this whole experience to a higher level, almost sacramental then, when one is blessed to make the life journey with a true love. It is to no avail to make the journey with less.

Wherever this is read, whoever reads my words, know this to be so...... a true destined lover once found is the greatest joy of all. No passion can equal the connection that is felt then. NO words can describe the passion that is felt and experienced with the receipt of a true love. One only has to experience the sensation to know the joy of it. It is the greatest of all gifts. The heart knows the way. Find your mates and find your special dreams that will all come true. Learn to trust and believe that it is so.

It is the matter of believing that needs repair. It is our lack of believing in all things temporal as they stand, as if that could not be changed with our hearts. Believe me when I tell you, there is no greater teacher than the teacher from your heart. No greater gifts to share than the gifts of love, one to the other. No greater thing upon the Earth than the expansion of consciousness towards the love of humanity and the spirit of caring and growing wiser in the presence of our Higher - Self, acknowledged each and every day.

This, then, is the greater wisdom. But do not despair, as wisdom is a thing to be gotten daily. Things will come to us, and quickly so, if you would ready your wills, if you will open yourselves to the myriad possibilities. If you would follow your hunches, your higher, intuitive instincts and be led to your mates…trust and go. Trust and move. Trust what it is that we know intuitively and move on that. Do not question what would come to us, seemingly, naturally. We are closer to the truth if we would be simple and accept some things, easily as so. There is no lack but the lack within our souls to perceive what is so incredible…that we will live on and on and on through to this vast continuum. ***SO MOTE IT BE.***

All secondary in consideration, after our love mate has crossed over again, all time that is left is the time for the remaining spouse/soul to further mature and no time should be lost in adapting to these new facts: that we are ageless in truth; our bodies will change; and that with each life we will have a new body, giving up that old body when we cross. And once out of the physical plane, we will fill life again in the Spirit! That life is good also, the soul adapting once again to life on this side, without a human body.

This is a repeating theme and very few, unless mediums, understand the truth of these things, as mediums have the ability to move through the window of time, going backwards and forward, to scan for what information it is that they need for their pursuit of writing or knowledge, or in simple readings for the immediate help of the person in front of them, seeking help in some personal matter.

It is the thing to remember and to learn from lifetime to lifetime. That yes, it does matter. What we do, say, and think and the reverse of that…all of it does matter. So indeed, always try to do your best. Don't let a day go by without putting yourself into it. Finish your dreams, your goals and *strive to the utmost to better the lives of all* that know you and all that love you.

If there are children and grandchildren, and the remaining spouse is situated financially, then the remaining love mate may have the opportunity to help and guide the youngest of family members around themselves. They can bless their family group with all their sacred acquired wisdom. And this is a magnificent ending to any life, a pearl to be acquired. There is no greater thing to permit and encourage than acts of love and caring, whether family, friends, or humanity at large. All people will benefit from constant rejuvenation of the Spirit.

Likewise, to embrace again upon the road of a career that was not finished from a prior history of advancing one's talents, is another choice, another path to walk upon. Time could be well spent here, finishing up one's life in the course of study within the field of one's level of intense interest. This further develops the mind and will contribute to all focus in future lifetimes, as none of this newly acquired skill is lost but gathered and saved in synopsis fashion in the seed atoms at the end of each lifetime, refined and integrated into the existing overview of files, as discussed in earlier chapters on the operating system, the Higher – Self.

The practice of life is the practice of moving on and embracing the many possibilities that will then present themselves around any individual that finds them in this situation, the situation of life and living.

In any case, rejuvenation and reconciliation are still the messages from the soul. We simply must go on with our lives wherein we find ourselves. There is but to go on and to re-inspire all that we embrace with our thoughts, our deeds and our raising of consciousness, and our efforts to love and participate with each other.

That is the larger role. There may be no physical retreat. We must come forward and participate in order to fulfill our destinies with each other. And this is the nature of humanity, *a Spirit that needs constantly to commune*. A Spirit that needs very much to love and be loved; one to the other, across all segments of time and space, in related and unrelated environments, rejuvenating our Spirits through the ongoing processes, the ongoing opportunities of reconciliation.

CHAPTER SIXTEEN

ADDICTIONS, ABUSE, BEHAVIORAL MANIFESTATIONS AND DISORDERS OF THE BRAIN

ADDICTIONS in the United States and around the globe are staggering, troublesome problems for the nature of humanity. Humanity is not prepared for the manifestations of the brain that occur when a person introduces the brain to the state of euphoria that often accompanies the misuse of drugs, narcotics, and other things such as alcohol, induced into the pathways of the brain through the vital organ delivery system.

Once the brain has been introduced to these chemicals, addiction can begin swiftly. For some, the very first use of alcohol sets the stage for a lifetime pattern of abuse. It is even more difficult to refuse the likes of heroin or other forceful drugs once introduced to the entity. The initial feelings created in the brain are such that the brain will automatically set up a new file and start to request the very thing introduced to it. This is a symptom of pathology of the functioning of the brainwave systems.

Much of the human body is run autonomically by the brain system. This is a naturally corresponding system, created to be governed by the Higher – Self-management program; induction through the use of drugs and chemicals in the body can overrule the monitor. Drugs and chemicals excite and induce the brain to function beyond the range of behavior it was designed to work at in a basic, everyday, "balanced fashion" for best occupational results, i.e. SURVIVAL!

Therein is the problem. It is difficult to return to basic living after the entity has been introduced to the euphoric state and excitement of high biology through drugs. The focus of the brain is then disturbed and under the influence of the chemicals. Leadership that was designed to come in through the Higher - Self program is then disrupted, as it is hard to reach the entity in the basic ways. The person that is suffering the addiction becomes non-responsive in an ordinary manner and difficult to lead and exhibit self- control.

Exhibitions of the troublesome nature created is best demonstrated in the rate of abuse and disorderly behavior patterns and conditions that incur in the lives of those involved with these high inflammatory drugs and patterns of addictions relating to substance abuse of all kinds.

You may ask why the attraction? For those that have not tried this level of chemistry the attraction is not understood. Perhaps it is easier to understand *if each person would think of one thing, they most desire to have in an over-balanced manner.* Think of that one thing and how hard it is to resist the temptation to have it in quantity beyond what you know is good and normal usage; then you will begin to understand the impulsive nature of human chemistry.

Undeniably tempting, are some of these intoxicants! It is better not to know some things; but simply not go there in any extreme or exposed fashion. Whatever it is you desire, watch for early warning signs of the beginning of the symptoms of pathology. This is the best teaching accord you can challenge yourself with; that you should ask of yourself to be in balance always. That is the best place for you to function from; a balanced person does not abuse anything or anyone. The focus is on attunement in all regards, in all parts of a person's life.

Expressions that would lead one in either direction, either too much of a thing or not enough, are then part of the mind's discernment program. We are teaching our brains constantly and updating our brains with new thoughts daily. Appreciable differences can occur as this system was designed to be a flawless, timeless, gatherer and delineator of new information that comes through the senses and is then systematically applied for usage through the brain function systems. As soon as that new data is entered into the thought stream it is disseminated through the brain files quickly and placed in the right file for processing, saving, and immediate access.

When we understand this format, we will be more careful in what we allow to repeat through our brains. This is why old habits are hard to break. The operational system, the Higher – Self, is not understood in its breath and magnitude of abilities. This system would not work if it were not able to function through many lifetimes in this manner. Therefore, it must always be a learning machine *with spiritual leadership at the helm.*

The operating system, the Higher- Self, will balance the new data that it receives daily. It receives the data files from many sources, as it will pick up information in an individual fashion, as well as a collective fashion. I am making a reference to the astral plane, where the soul receives its fresh charge of energy as it sleeps and downloads communal information that comes to it spiritually.

Now we wish to continue with the subject of how the mind works and what causes disruption and behavioral discords.

Now you may ask exactly how does this process of disruption begin and I would say here, easily so. Often, too easily, and the brain can begin its repetitive need for a drug, distillation alcohol, or other addictive action, on a daily basis, rather quickly. As the drug, alcohol or addictive action hits the brain, the brain is establishing an immediate tolerance for what it intakes, as the brain is connecting to the substance and the action that is surrounding the action tied to the addictions.

All addictions are tied to the pleasure centers in the brain that connect to the mind. These pleasure centers are sensory. Each center has its established level to perform in normal balance. However, ingesting of substances that produce euphoria takes the brain to the new level of experience, a new rate of change. The brain will experience the pleasure, change the set point and want to re-experience what it has found at the higher, increased level in its file. It then takes over and will request relief to this level once it has been introduced to this level. Any action that is introduced to the system that is pushed into extreme will create a new file and reestablish a place, a node, changing the prior response calibration, set points and set up of the body monitoring system.

The Higher - Self will try to reassert itself for guidance but once the pattern gets a strong hold on the individual, the entity gets out of the normal range of regulation and then begins the process where it is harder to maintain control of the daily life by the Higher - Self management system.

Free will! Choices! This is why the entire soul must have the final control and say and be the chief resource and challenger of all of our actions and choices if we are to live well and be happy with ourselves in our lives.

Initially, the beginnings of a bad habit may be hard to detect, as often this is misleading. Individuals often think they can stop using their drug of choice, or action of choice, anytime they want; that they are *not attached* to their habit. The feeling is to continue on with usage, or repeat our bad actions, as the entity enters the field of denial and will not identify or give-up its pleasure pursuit and experience. The truth of this is that it is a problem and the problem will be ongoing and cause pain and suffering, as the addicted entity gets further down the road with the addiction.

This establishes individual and family behavioral dysfunctions. These conditions are passed through to the children of the addicted with predisposed conditions as presets in their DNA chain, if applicable. This tendency to preset in the genes is also true in the consideration of other factors such as tendencies to overeat coming from fat cell records in the pattern of the parents of the children, wherein obesity was pronounced.

The family involved with the person who has the addiction then suffers the consequences of the person's actions. This can cause many problems with marital life and one's livelihood. It can further itself with ruination if addictive behavioral conditions are left unchecked, untreated by medical professionals, over the course of a lifetime.

The tie-in to physical abuse against women and children is directly related to the tendency of the brain to react suddenly as it increases its cortical pressure in the head area and causes anger to occur completely unannounced; often times, rage comes on in a violent outburst of energy. What is actually happening is an interior response reaction occurring in the mid-brain that is tied to the disruptions. The mind needs to experience, in expectorant-like fashion, a way to, spit-out, drive-out of the body the portion that is the problem, as it cannot be released through the head in a normal fashion. Addictions give rise to disruptive behavioral outbursts induced by drug conditions, which drugs, commonly speaking, would not be in the body, causing erratic responses, were the entity not addicted.

Misuse of prescription drugs can be fatal if the person is not guided to the truth in these matters. They also can cause addictive conditions. Palpitations of the heart, arrhythmia, caused by some drugs, can cause fatal heart attacks as some drugs cause contractions in the heart valves, veins and arteries leading into the pathways of the heart support system.

Although medical science is much better today than it ever was, it still is in the infancy stages of where it will be over the course of the future. In the future many drugs will be eliminated, as the prescribed treatments will be more of a spiritual nature, given prior to the arrival of any tendency to illness. These things are of the future in medical history books that we see here from our use of the advanced astral projection methods. We work at these things on the spiritual level in order to help humanity in the future. This is the way the two worlds work together, although little is written or truly known about these facts and procedures.

We wish to say here that smoking also qualifies as an addiction and also the use of sex for purposes that are nonproductive and not clearly prescribed for lovemaking also can become addictive behavioral patterns, equally as disruptive in life as the other kinds of addictions that we have mentioned on these pages.

Let us begin here with why? This is the brain …the brain system is a learning system. We are teaching it and educating it daily. All foods and liquids that enter our bodies are affecting its normal balancing. The water intake in our bodies is always fluctuating. The absolute control is the factor of assimilation and management of all functions through the oversight of the Higher-Self, which is programmed to regulate all functions. Almost the entire daily functioning that the human being is experiencing in the course of the normal day, is work performed through this autonomic response system.

When we place foods into our bodies that are not good for us, we leave ourselves open to imbalances in our chemistries. This chemistry that is kept within our bodies is changing daily in coordination to what we ingest and experience through our vital organs. Therefore, what we *ingest* and *experience through our bodies* is important. Raw foods are best and liquids that are clear are best. All else is a matter of taste and personal choices.

We do not mean that food is not good. But, many of the foods today that the public intakes are loaded with chemicals and refinements that are not easily assimilated and processed through the body, leaving a residue in our veins and bloodstreams that cause blockages and stores of ready fat that are then carried on reserve in the body. Nutritional values are lost as the body continues to store that which will not be deleted. Through the body fat, the stagnation effect comes into play, as the humans today are not matching their intakes; with caloric consumption too high and the offsets in outputs to energy units not in the corrective ratio to work properly and produce optimum health results.

Therefore, the modern human body is not functioning at top performance and must adapt to meet the rash induction of forceful things added to the system, which things are making the system harder to manage. As the heart and valves of the body are forced to carry more weight, the preponderance of obesity upon the planet increases and shows the entire point I am making here. The results are not the signs of optimum healthy bodies and life conditions.

The human body needs less artificial intake of all sorts. Increase the natural food intake and limit alcohol use for best results; then the daily, healthier patterns we establish for ourselves will produce less fat and fatigue for our bodies.

In our daily lives, humanity needs to consider all things with an *overview* placed highly in the center of the mind. The first question of everyday should be…*why do I exist?* All other questions should come in after that. This first point brings solace to the soul daily. If we can address the first prime issue and run this higher thought through our brains, then we can address our bodies and direct our energies in what we do with purpose. *If we have no overview of our lives in place*, then each new day starts and ends as before and we that have been human would say to you there, that the *overview is* the directive from the soul which needs to run the engine in the body system. The key to the car, Madame, is to understand why we are in the car! This is a serious point of meditation.

Each day we should meditate sincerely on what we are doing in our bodies' and with our bodies. We should ask our Higher-Self to help and to guide us actively. We should be developing our will power each and every day. We should be able to say "no" to all areas of abuse or addictions in our lives. To do so, we need to develop a strong willpower base. This is best developed by the higher mind but the higher mind must first buy the concept.

The overview is presented to the lower mind from the higher vehicle, the Higher – Self guide. If you pay attention, it is trying to filter through new instructions daily. If we don't listen, then we do not get the benefit of the guidance coming from above.

Stressing our body and mind is not an active, healthy method of living and we need to learn to manage ourselves better in all that we are doing. In many cases we can teach ourselves better methods of treatment for our ills and the conditions that are driving us crazy. But we need to take responsibility and make the effort!

Mental sicknesses of all types and degree are increasing upon the Earth, conditions becoming more pronounced as the chemicals in the air and the environment are unfriendly to the human body which is absorbing more than is being calculated and understood by the Earth plane science and medical communities today. This is a big reason that so many are getting ill with the diseases of cancer and other diseases on the increase because of dangerous environmental conditions that are not being dealt with or even properly gauged.

Chemically fed animals that are then consumed by humans in quantity are also a part of the problem and a contributing cause of illness, obesity, clogged arteries leading to heart problems, stroke, and many other responses of the body to over-extended conditions, over-taxed internal, and poorly functioning operational systems within the body.

The Higher - Self is attuning to the down pouring of love and energy from this side. If asked to access that pool of continual energy, it will greatly enhance our lives with stronger happiness, possible through better choices made through better communication skills with others and ourselves in our world. Then the world affairs will not bog us down so. We will be teaching our brains to go to the higher overview and when we do that in all actions, the governor – our own internal regulator, will come in to monitor our actions and we will get the help that we need then to resist the addictions and stop all abuse.

This condition of repetitive action on the part of the brain goes the entire way back to the ancient times when the group soul ruled the souls upon the Earth. This was a time when our Higher – Self vehicles were in their infancy and so our developmental schedule was primal. Upon the Earth, at that time, group souls existed. Souls were guided much as the animals are still guided now.

Individual consciousness comes out of the group soul. The group soul aspect is part of the history of the developing sentient higher being that is humanity today. However, the basic needs of the societies were met through the leadership coming in from the group soul, direction from a guiding Spirit force that is always there in the beginning phases of nascent humankind. If it were not so, humanity would not be where it is today.

Over eons of time individual ego, freewill and thought streams were separated out from the group, because humanity had reached the stage where the evolving development of the brain made it possible to survive on their own without the guardian light forces guiding them safely.

This is part of the problem today…. The shift to push into excitement that the brain is not prepared to manage is to tap into evolvement that is primal.

In the beginning, pleasure was for procreation. Children were necessary for the growth and continuation of humanity upon the planet. The Creator designed the male and female attraction, with that in mind.

Today the advent of recreational sex with no purposes of procreation, *presents the brain with reflections of running in the wild*, a style of living that it has long since given up because it has risen to intelligent living, which intelligence of the brain would dictate our actions be reasonable and balanced.

These extremes cause the brain to reflect upon the wild, animalistic, most primal desires of humanity that have been put to rest, or at least driven into submission by choice of the soul, in order to advance humanity into its next level of ascendance. **This is why all extremes of any kind are to be avoided.**

Reflections of the past will come in and ignite our animalistic natures - these natures no longer being necessary as having been given up long ago to a better process; through spiritual reality above the animals. The encased brain is challenged always with the next level of ascendance, where humanity is required to leave the vestiges of our later stages behind and ascend to something better.

It cannot be emphasized enough that love of our mate is essential to our overall wellness and happiness. Conditions of stress that are within so many marriages today are at the root of marital problems. Today's world is translated as complicated, too much so we say. Our impatience, anxiety and lack of consideration for others in general, speak to our state of mind.

Creating blissfulness with one's partner is of the highest order of things to accomplish while married. An active sexual life assures a balance of both partners if this love is part and parcel to all lovemaking that occurs with the couple. Forgiveness of all transgressions is the key. Ability to commit to stay within the relationship established for all sexual desire and release of energies, along with commitment in the partnership with honesty and affection are essentials, if a marriage is to remain solid.

Sexual gratification by marital partners outside of the marriage is a thing to be avoided. Lust and sexual depravity will lead to the destruction of the family and increased disease.

Today the world is being filled with heightened sensuality like never before. The methods of communication have filtered through the minds of humanity taking it off course with these energies, presented many times with explicit sensuality pushed to the extreme and shown without regard to connectedness, respect, or love between men and women. As this action ties into the most primal need of men and women, it can be addictive and lead beyond the visual presentation to the desire to do the thing that is watched, heard, or received in some other sensory form.

In the beginning of this chapter I spoke of staying within balance. Many things can become addictive, the addictive nature of what is tried and experienced through sensory inputs and outputs, being completely underrated and misunderstood.

The nervous system will reflect with anxiousness and lack of satisfaction as we increase our intake of all things carnal, physically craved and experienced in the extreme, producing damage to ourselves as our spirituality can only suffer with this exposure.

Just as with drugs, sexual addiction can start as a small view and soon turn into a thing that is overwhelming to the senses as we are inducing ourselves, down the road, to an extreme experience. The mind is an aggressive thing when it is attuning to a primal reflection, whose nature is carnal and which will pull us backwards; animalistic natures are difficult to resist under temptation and the pull of repetitive action.

The need to repeat the action is addictive. Experienced, it is difficult to turn away and not do a thing that is impressed upon the mind to repeat. The response will be to seek relief at the higher frequency wherein the pleasure was experienced and the entity will be drawn to that experience in order to have the pleasure repeated. There is no satiety, which is not temporal. We will be drawn again and again to repeat that experience in order to have the pleasure repeated. This condition of addictive behavior can jump sectors and make its way into other areas in the soul's life, producing out of control desires of the flesh and even lead it to dual addictions.

In today's highly advanced technological world, you would think that people would have more respect for what they invite into their lives. We see this as a troublesome problem now for this world. That in fact, it is encouraging itself into things, which are not good for advancement but surely readying the soul for going backwards! We will speak more of the brain and the other conditions of living in the remaining chapters of this, our first book, from the Astara, Highlands- Central, above the Earth's atmosphere, working in conjunction with our scribe, Mrs. Lindsay.

CHAPTER SEVENTEEN

MANSIONS OF PROSPERITY, MANIPULATION OF GRAVITY, SCIENTIFIC FRONTIERS, AND OUTER SPACE!

TO BEGIN WITH, this chapter will deal with the advances into Space that will come to this Planet Earth. Advances are based on our current projections and considerations, from the review of the overall status of the world today, *as it is.*

The comparison to that review is the point at which the people of Earth have achieved the stage of growth across broad fronts of intelligence gatherings, which will make these advancements possible. Advancements, wherein they will attain the abilities to decipher the necessary links in the chain of discoveries that will make long range outer space travel inevitable!

We wish to add here, right at the start of this chapter, that the spiritual level of the planet will have greatly advanced mankind as well as maturing it to the point wherein *trustworthiness to enter the universe in depth is rewarded.* Young planets are guided to this stage and watched closely so as not to be released to the wider universe when they are not ready to do so. These guideposts are things not realized now, on your Earth plane. Today, on Earth, many doubt the very existence of God. We say that wisdom will show that the entire universe is guided from the very first breath of creation. It is a great honor to speak of Him here as we move forward with this chapter on expansion!

Those of us that have gone beyond your planet know this to be so and respect this fact: *the first principal of existence is the existence of the Godhead and that all else stems from the derivation of that sole fact.* There is no world if there is no Godhead. Those that have surpassed the intelligence quotient of the Earth plane do not question this mighty consideration as if an aphorism, but show it the respect that it warrants as an unwavering tenet, in fact.

As the people of Earth reach the stage of acknowledgement of the soul within the body and reasoning power to respect what has been given, then the universe will open wider beyond the level of considerations that are in place in your world now. Choosing the path of ascendancy means leaving our old bad habits behind. The three things, major points for humanity to leave behind, are: intolerance, injustice and greed for self-aggrandizement in all forms. These are major challenges for humanity to overcome and master upon the Planet Earth.

The characteristics of the heart of man will have to change, as it is stubbornness that leaves with it a sadness of war through the ages and still no peace, if not changed.

The true war is the war between man and his heart or the lack of his heart involved in all of his actions and considerations with himself and the world he lives in and all that is in the world with him. This world has been given to him to shepherd and humanity cannot move ahead without bringing all of its many peoples alongside. All differences must be overcome to see the prevailing wisdom of these words. War of our physical parts must end. There is no other way. Your world must learn this truth before venturing into maturity, which is the universe beyond your Earth plane; deep, long-range space travel being the beginning stage into that maturity.

The first link in this chain of discovery is the manipulation of gravity. These things, these understandings of exigent mathematics, must come to Earth before there will be deep, outer space travel in air conveyances of a different type required to pass through the outer galaxies unimpaired by the conditions presented there, which conditions are formidable. Outer space being defined in this context: all known areas of the universe that are not known to your world today. There are many portals to pass through in looking at the universe.

The manipulation of gravity cannot come until the understanding of the true nature of the universe is derived. It is not possible to come to those understandings without a complete change and broadening of the scope of mathematics and the correlatives to this subject. New subjects will come to fruition named accordingly, as they are discovered. Subjects need to be understood by the science world in order to reach the mental capacity to bring into reality the new tools and designs necessary to make these hardwire discoveries possible on Earth. These things are of the future. One day at a time.

Before that happens, the advance into *quantum physics* brings with it many new discoveries which will lead naturally into the discoveries that will open the door to the possibility of space travel and time travel within the body as well, while not actually moving the body from the place where it is. This we call "medium travel". "Medium travel" gives the operator of the body the opportunity to go ahead into the future and see what is to come, as well as to go backward to see what was; these gifts are not of your time but will be coming to a few, as the true nature of the communication with us on this side becomes known.

As of this writing, a few have the gift of communication with us *exparte,* by that we mean a direct connection with us on this side. (You, Mrs. L., are one of these selected for this gift.) Now there are others on the planet at this time that also have the "gift" and are working with other master teachers. Communication there is also resulting in books covering other subjects than what this Brotherhood will cover here with you.

The understanding of mathematics is much larger than the known documentation that is employed by your Earthian studies. The amplitude of studies of the galaxies is much larger. These studies are larger fields of endeavors, but we see that these advances will come to Earth, as the scientific groups are studying hard on the Earth to make progress and be the first to pioneer through the outer reaches of space.

Material discernment of all the components that are required to move from your current realm of physicality to materials and devices needed to travel through space will be derived most accurately by those that are in the vanguard of the ongoing process of acquiring this basic acumen of mental fortitude. Let truth lead your scientific groups and truth of these matters will open the door to a more challenging realization of what is desired. Truth must be at the forefront in the hearts and souls of mankind. The messenger has the song but until the music has been heard we are stuck with yesterday's old hit parade. Focus and concentration are required to bring forward what is only perceived in its infancy by the few, the larger audience having not heard even a lilting effect of the new music drifting in, outdating the old.

So large is this desire, "the desire to know", that many will never stop even if your space center in Florida is closed, as scheduled. The world of scientific discovery will continue to be sponsored and funded in large part by medical industries that are now making breakthroughs in the inner workings of the body. Many leaps of a large magnitude will further this desire, for the conquest of outer space is every bit as strong as the desire to know the medical answers to the problems of the body and therein create the solutions for humanity.

These solutions are well sought after by the medical pharmacology types that desire to gain this information in order to create *their mansions of prosperity.* The desire to increase, as in the wealth of the nations, is a catalyst for change all over the planet. Although this is not the target of the success, it is many times the reason, the prime reason for taking on the risks implied in the endeavors.

Billions of dollars are put into these fields of discoveries so that the advances can produce medical cures in the way of medical drugs, new patents on medical appliances, medical breakthrough surgical techniques, and machines to assist in operations on the human body.

These fields are broad and will grow broader over time as the universe is a large place and must have refined senses in order to be approached; whether our science officers will take us there first or our pure undertakings from the engineering side that move from basic aviation that exists now, into the material findings that make space gravitational application of field theories regarding life possible. We must say that this will change your planet for the better, propelling humankind to other planets and places for both visitation and colonization.

Colonization is of the future and will maximize the existence of humankind through the universe. There are planets that will come of age wherein life can exist. These planets are myriad beyond the scope of your existing tools of metrics or devices to see their very existence. Even so, they are there as you are there on the Earth only able to see as far as your scientific tools allow you to do so. One day these things will change, as civilization is required to grow and move ahead. It is the job of the light forces that work with the planets to help and assist the people of the existing civilization being guarded and guided to move ahead as quickly as we can ascertain that it is safe to help them do so.

Life on other planets exists. But that life is not the subject for this book. Suffice it to say that each planet is in its beginning stages of development and that we work on these things for eons of time and when they are ready, life will come about and then the process begins all over again. This is the way of guardianship. You are not alone there although we cannot be seen by most, unless they are mediums. Even then the gifts vary and not all mediums have the same gift in prescient terms.

The work of the mediums in the future will bring with it the responsibility to guide those that are to benefit and receive the information. This will become a highly trusted position. Clarity of receipt will require the best minds that are to be maintained for these purposes. They will be protected and held in safe keeping so as not to be disturbed in any way by the daily trends of the world as it is not possible to transport this information easily if the entity is distracted with the daily minutia of the day.

The medium must guard against all those that would impose on her, otherwise the energy field gets disturbed and then the portal effect cannot be refined. By this we mean that consciousness of the entity cannot be melded in such a way to attune with us easily. Temperament and body temperature must be exactly right. Anger and emotional outbursts of all sorts will have a negative pull on the medium and the very health of the being can be damaged.

Outside conditions of the planet can also have a disrupting effect making transmission through various weather conditions very difficult if not impossible to achieve. We take all these things into consideration before we attempt communication and will break off communication from this side with our mediums when conditions are not true to form as required for proper delivery of the information from this side. In this way we work and will prevail thereafter, for our thoughts will be left with the medium, for any necessary corrections to the script that we dictated. All of these things are part of a working convention that is established with us and this is how this task is accomplished between the Spirit- side and the Earth plane side.

The sensitivity required for this job is high. Otherwise it is not possible to hear us. But we compensate as we attune to the medium exactly and try to bring up the soul to this level. We do not tune down. The medium is bought up to us to allow the transmission to go forward. This is a highly sophisticated thing to be accomplished and if the mind of the person attuning is not strong, the words will not be brought through correctly.

Very few can hear us; those that do must work with us to become clairvoyants of a higher measure than they started out with, having the native ability to do this job from birth. Such is the case here with you, Madame. Our mission is to increase the strength and abilities required so that we can improve the methods in which we work with you. Then the process can be repeated, safety measures always taken into consideration as the overall health and well-being of the soul; the station on Earth being our first and foremost concern.

We do not always succeed with our mission. Many times, the person has so much going on in their life that they cannot give the time and energy to enforce the discipline required to show and record the words correctly. This is a long process and the will must be strong to withstand the thoughts and other things that come in to steal away the time and efforts that would be required to do this book.

Persistence is key to this process. Belief that we are real is required also as any doubt of that will inhibit the medium and eventually the desire required to function will be lost to the fear or the consequences of the action that may come into the applicant's mind.

Fear appears again and again. I have said in an earlier chapter regarding fear that this is the reason most people do not get whatever it is they seek. Fear stops them and hurdles them to the ground. The doors that would open will not be opened. The connections to others in the world that would have come into that person's life will not come as the fear will so inhibit their thoughts and actions. Confusion will cloud the thought stream and the *opportunity* to find the right path to choose which will lead to the person, place, or thing that was to come in and help the entity – will be lost. Good instructions to lead to the area of succession will not be found and progress may be seriously delayed, diminished or even forfeited.

I wish to repeat again that our thoughts are energy, live energy. This is why humanity must strive to think correctly and use its thought repeating process correctly to the advantage of itself, lifting itself out of all forms of negativity.

The thought streams of so many there on Earth are clouded over with failures recorded in the past and still repeated in the mind and then standing in the way of daily progress. We must train ourselves to get beyond whatever is holding us down or back. We must learn to teach ourselves to ascend, not regress. Regressive behavior brings with it the sadness that is reaped by affirming again our losses or lack of victory. I have touched on these things in an earlier chapter.

I wish to say *further that it is so even with a true love, which would come to us.* We can simply *stand in the way* of him or her and then we miss the destined person coming into our lives altogether. Believing makes it possible. If we do not believe, if we are highly resistant to even the consideration of true love, it is nearly impossible to connect with that would-be-lover, and create a mansion of prosperity. Life, then, becomes a difficult thing. The tendency then will be to marry for convenience or conventional reasons and this is one of the main causes for the effect of divorce. Divorce rates being so high in the world at this time; it is better to wait for the exact one than to settle for less and end up in dead end marriages.

Without our compatible love mate, we have a harder life alone; sharing is important, as the human soul is a cooperative Spirit that needs to make a home together with others, *not separate from others.* The very Spirit of humanity is *communal, collective* in its design as that design was necessary for primal survival, as recorded through history.

If we did not have that, the Spirits in community, set in the human brain as a primal need, then humanity would not be able to advance in the future, as much that is done on the planet is done with groups and although individual leadership is at the helm, it is a core group of workers that come in behind the efforts and leadership of the group and complete the tasks under development.

The growth of the human mind is a story in itself as it is, mechanically, a progressive design, leaving room in the head construct for the add-ons that will come to the design within the scope of the outline that was set in the beginning. Nothing stays the same. Everything is in progress. Whether seen or unseen, all things are moving ahead. This is the way of the nature of all things whether animal, mineral, or any other biologically expressed thing, human or otherwise in composition, on the planet.

The universe is a dictionary of magnificence that is very broad, your planet being just one of the views to admire. The scope of this consideration is huge and not put into any book that is in your world at this time. We wish to explain in synopsis, the following: At this time of writing, these things are not yet realized upon the Earth plane: *That there is no division from our side to your side that would stop true communication.* However, we have not the authority to merge the two sides. This authority rests beyond us and we are but in authorship of nothing as you on the Earth also are but re-inventors of all the plans and efforts already written by the Creator. Were we to accept this truth, much of what holds us back on Earth would disappear in our minds, as the bright light of this first principal truth would overshadow all with energetically rooted confidence, dismissing our doubts.

It is still the pride of man that keeps him happy in ignorance and impressed too easily by the things he creates. We say that these creations are *but play things* in the mind of the Creator who is to begin with infinite, having existed always. We know of no time that He did not exist. He is the prime number. He is the beginning of all beginnings, stretching through all the history of histories. This world is goaded into pride again and again being wrapped up constantly with its merger creations, creations that would not have come about *without the Creator putting all things into motion*. His authority supersedes any authority upon the Earth.

It is necessary to repeat here that religious ideologies are now holding back humanity in the respect to unity. All need to come to the understanding that there are many paths to the Creator and that there was infinite reasoning in the creation of diversity. That to see the Creator from various perspectives was in His plan, not without His plan; that there is no need or requirement to merge all into one religion. That each religion has its necessary part and that is also part of His plan. That we would have to come to balance with each other's chosen hierarchy is also part of the plan. Both sides, the negative and the positive in life, are necessary. That it is provided for us and that all we need is to be conscious of it and be happy within our structures and try to amend our countries into alignment, representing goodness and liberty for all. That goodness is the essence and virtue on the path, *the path available to all*. Reaching for these understandings is ready, credible knowledge available to humankind, right now, within this very instant.

To war over our differences because of the precepts that we hold dear within our religious understandings is not the solution for humanity. Defensively proceeding against our neighbors on foreign shores that do not think as we do is not the answer. Even then, we must show goodness and virtue in how we manage ourselves. Annihilation is not the answer unless you want war upon the Earth from one faction against another, forever!

To begin with, all religious have some part of it right, some redeeming glimmer of the truth of the Godhead. But there are variants in all the books. Were you to view what is at the core of the books and forget the rhetoric then you might do better in how you live with each other there upon the Earth plane.

There is knowledge of the Creator EVEN with those *that have never heard His word*. There is no missionary outpost required, for these tribes are now, at this time in the world, quickly losing their spots, their territory upon the planet, as the tribal fathers cannot hold on to the land because others will seize the land for commerce, running the native people into extinction. Being "more civilized" does not denote seizing other's lands – but is a contradiction to it! This is a point of meditation and a firm reality check!

As this happens, the people indigenous to that area of the world will be forced out. If unwilling, with no human oversight from a governing body providing protection, rule and order of law and civil authority, these tribes will be shoved off the land, even killed or maimed, by invading parties, determined to conquer the land. This is still the way of forceful foreclosure by brutal people, puppets of tyrannical rule, that are this very moment subjecting others to abuse of all sorts, while prevailing in the sub-Sahara deserts of Africa and other regions upon the Earth, lands that are lesser known to most people of the western world of civilized thought.

Refugee camps are growing as we are writing here today, proof of the things I am saying which are still in the world today, un-abating, un-abolished upon the Earth. It is still *ruthlessness* at the helm for so many and selective intervention by the rest of the world, doling out money after the fact, in foreign aid, after the genocide has occurred to masses of people eliminated without mercy in the most horrible manner of death and destruction, *not imagined* murder but murder made real by bloody thugs, carrying out acts of rapacious greed for control. Rwanda, Africa and the overt massacre of over one million people there is a prime example. History is replete with many other examples of the same, deplorable events repeating upon the Earth plane, where there was no collective intervention by the rest of the world powers to stop these tragedies of massive genocide!

Building mansions of prosperity will not bring settlement and universal happiness to mankind if in creating these cultures we have engaged in force, killing, mergers of corruption and other co- tortured methods implored in order to reach our immediate goals of satisfaction to our bank coffers. Time and time again we are held back by what is not addressed. We then spend our time in slavery to the thought of creation of worlds where the true nature and Godlike quality innate in mankind is driven underground. Our lives are then in commitment to maintaining our mansions of prosperity, each soul creating his own world to the extent of his Earthly wherewithal to bring in his thought forms of a plutocratic type, into a creation around himself.

Whereas, we would like to say… whether it is found in outer space or whether it is found on the Planet Earth, the truth of all of these things must be recognized and acknowledged. Only then can lasting happiness proceed sincerely for mankind. Wars and agendas of thieving will continue to rob the Planet Earth of its best yet plan, the plan of ascendancy, wherein we are required to leave the vestiges of our old bad habits behind and grow into the future stronger and brighter within our governed humanity, where our soul nature will implore us to reach beyond our greed.

It is not material wealth that our soul is reaching for but the spiritual side of man's nature, much in total denial, today. This world lives with pain and suffering coming from many areas of denial, which have at the core, the denial of the Spiritual- side. It is spirituality that will bring man out into the universe where the outer space travel will reveal that the hand of the Creator was also at work there, painting the universe with a wide array of other planets, other considerations. This is not the end all, be all, here on this page, as there is much more to say later. For today, this is what we think and impart to humanity. Bring peace within your day.

CHAPTER EIGHTEEN

SUBJUGATION OF THE CONSCIOUSNESS FROM WITHIN: REPRESSION

TO BEGIN WITH, abhorrent behaviors in a civilized world, such as criminality, murder, torture, rendition of tyranny, nation between nations, for the purposes of performance of torture, by governments, western or otherwise, are all forms of the subjugation of the consciousness from within, repression of the soul.

No matter how distinguished you might be with your letters and diplomas, you cannot elude your true selves. You might fool others and impress many with your outer selves, but your soul level knows your true colors. The Higher - Self is the Oversoul of all humans, each human possessing one of these as a guiding operational system, functioning throughout the brain system for any human lifetime. Whether folly or glory, it, the Higher - Self, keeps a record of all data encompassed in the life.

Awareness of this guiding force, this light of information, is a blessing when the soul comes to the point of being able to grasp its existence. Just the same it exists, whether the entity is aware of it or not. We have covered these basics in the earlier chapters. If you need to refresh yourselves, please return to re-read those earlier chapters before reading any further, as what I will be explaining next is beyond that preliminary information. These will be the areas of expansion for this chapter.

Now, upon the Earth much is made of freedom, rights and liberties of citizenry of nations, some nations having given "more power to the people" than others. Much is made of it, homage paid too often in lip service without the feeling of reverence that is due. Have you forgotten your past? Have you forgotten the price you paid for your freedom and liberties? Are the pains of the struggle put aside with preference given to every form of escapism, every form of alleviation or attachment to consciousness as to where you are as a civilization in the world? Perhaps these things are things to pass on to your politicians? Responsibilities you need to put in their bailiwick . . . a burden to throw at the foot of the Senate Chambers or a decision to be made at the helm of the congressional floor meetings? Always, it seems, you wish someone else to carry the water, someone else to carry the weight of freedom.

Today, fear is the smell in the air worldwide. As communication covers the globe the downloaded images that hit the people in the foreign lands are very discouraging to many. They see that the western world is different from their own. The news is often pointed within the direction of sovereignty of nations, voices rolling off in expressions, which are not truthful, but engage in propaganda.

This Propaganda Agenda is directed at the public audience using agencies that abound with information from the outside areas beyond the control of their immediate public audience's ability to research the truth from the untruth presented. Once the grip of disinformation is seeded, the entire world is subject to the end result. It is difficult to believe in a world that is not aware of the truth, having no counterpoint, no media exchange, to determine or decipher it, one fact from the other.

Modes of transfer of information are uploaded and then downloaded with bias, putting pressure on the public that receives the information and creating new animosities from foreign channels. Disruption is often not caught by those that are receiving the data. The agencies of destructiveness are concealed behind the drama that unfolds over the airwaves and on the television screens. Explosive camouflage is often not perceived and the deceivers learn to become infiltrating professionals with lack of scruples and more in the business of getting their points of bias home to their immediate target audiences, often pitting the nations against themselves as "enemies". Disingenuousness all around!

It is the obligation of all citizens within all the countries that are free, to watch their public officials closely. Freedom is not freedom if tyranny is allowed to creep in through the back door. Ignorance or disinterest in accepting these facts as possibilities is tantamount to dropping your guard with weakness and inviting repression of freedom and liberties previous soldiers have fought and died for gallantly. You must *never allow* yourselves in your daily work world to become so exclusively caught up in its work-a-day material gatherings that you forget all else, that you forget the need for the existence of vigilance over your freedom and rights within your nations! Your native abilities must allow you to be given over to deep respect for that which your sons and daughters of liberty will have as their heritage, a heritage loved and held so dearly to your hearts in your lifetime, passed through to you from your parents.

Vaguely, the world is seen again and again failing to remember this weakness to paying due diligence to these civil responsibilities and then, unfortunately, paying the price later when the wars begin again, when a new tyrant appears *from out of the blue, (it seems), who brings the world again to the brink of disaster. The unthinkable then becomes a new world order with liberty and justice for all, again, in peril! How many times must you learn this lesson? How many times must you suffer so deeply?*

Often times now, with the populations upon the Earth, you see that beginnings of more nuclear power considerations are coming to the forefront. There is some time left but it is necessary to ask yourselves "what will you do?" Will you stand against the power to destroy, which is increasing on the planet? What will you do to stand against the rise and prospect of a heritage left to your youngsters, who are less free and less privileged to live in the *pursuit of happiness, a fortunate condition* that you lived within your lifetime? What will you give of yourselves to protect the countries that are not equal? What does it mean to you that are free? Are you the guardians of freedom, the stewards of liberty?

Where is the need? Is there a need to see others free and see a better world, a new world for your children, which will be brighter than the world as it exists now? In large measure, what do you feel you owe to your existence? I could go on and on with questions that I would raise with each of you that read this text but my point would be well taken here if you would see that these are things that you should all be thinking about, now! Now, while there is still a planet called Earth! While there is still the opportunity to change what must be changed and protect what you have gained over the course of many rounds of souls upon this great blue planet, the Planet of Earth.

Torture, rendition of torture, arrangements developed between nations to perform torture on foreign lands in secret and avoid detection, even in a military context, are all forms of *abhorrent behavior*. These conditions are deplorable and abuse is abuse no matter where or when it is performed. Yet today, even so, these state of affairs, ordered evil by people and nations between nations, are egregious. There is no contrition of heart for these things done, measures meted out under the disguise of power, with claims of necessity to act based upon national security of land, nations and people, sovereignty against sovereignty. These things, allowed to continue, will most assuredly lead to the devaluation of the human soul and this devaluation is exactly what must be avoided. Because we know that these codes are violent abhorrent behaviors and will set humanity back, we speak of them here, in this chapter. These atrocities must not be allowed to prevail.

As we have spoken in the previous chapters, the human mind is a learning machine, a sophisticated gathering device. It also translates what it perceives, instantly filing these new images and facts of abhorrent behaviors in the files that are then immediately updated. This is where the damage is stored and the correlations to abuse will travel *as if a virus* within the human collective. Instead of lifting up humanity, these deeds will increasingly weigh the objects down into the mire.

In a time when communication of evil and evil doers has never been broader, mass infiltration of images, words and deeds of violent reruns, repeating upon the human consciousness, frame after frame after frame upon the TV screens, will only further erode the mindset of the human beings that then *revise* their understanding as to what is *allowable. Degradation becomes normalization. Humanity is then softened, desensitized throughout the senses, as this degradation is repeated over the course of time and witnessed daily.*

The same thing is happening now with the Internet infiltration and penetration of the codes of violence that are coming over the computer screen and shared with great numbers of people accessing the system. The Internet is a plague to humanity if allowed to become a cesspool of human desires, released onto the public in a way that is deceptively enticing many times. What may appear to be good at first is not good later.

Once addicted to the exposure, the action orientation may consume like a raging fire, those who are caught up in it.

Many do not have the will power to walk away from their involvement and will join the crippling force that has consumed them. The plague grows and makes its way spreading throughout society and doing damage to new victims.

The devaluing and degradation of the human soul is as easy as that, as the true nature of the gathering capability of the human mind is not understood. These metaphysical understandings are not known to most people as most people do not know of the existence of the Oversoul, (the Higher–Self) and the magnificent guidance system that has been with humanity since the beginning of time and has been in existence with prior usage before this civilization of Earth; as other civilizations existed before yours, yet are far off into the universe, in other areas, out of the range of sight to your Planet Earth. Still it is so.

Repression is the subjugation of the consciousness from within. Suppressing what is the best within yourselves will only take you backwards. Encouraging your souls to grow is moving ahead and forward; letting yourselves go backwards is not the way to future prosperity but only the way to troubled waters again. *Tyranny must be fought.* You have it within yourselves always to be great, *to be kind*, to think of others as you think of yourselves. It is wise to want the best for everyone and then to put the day right in the knowledge that you have participated to the fullness of the day. At the end of the day you can then rest knowing that you lived well within that day. Within that one-day, if you have stretched out in that day, you have found many opportunities *to be kind in your work and in your play with others.* If, in any day, you have found that you created an environment that caused havoc for others, then you must immediately repair the wrong you have done. This sets the soul into a firm understanding that it creates what it DOES. Consequently, think about what you are creating in total.

You create with your bodies, your minds and your souls. You are rich in what you engage every day. You may not miss an opportunity to advance it, your enrichment, if you are at peace with advancement. Knowing that you can move ahead brings with it the responsibility to do so and then to apply yourselves in that advancement. Likewise, seeing that others can have a life and the means to seek advancement will help you also. As you grow, everything around you will grow. You become teachers with your words and your actions. Teachers mirror what good things where taught to them in their childhood, reflecting back with goodness to others in their adult lives.

But when you engage in the devaluing of your human dignities, you do not advance. Likewise, you will be mired in the rancorous behaviors that you bring out in yourselves. The nature of man can be kind or it can be unkind. It is for you to choose what you will become. Kindness is growth for the soul of the highest order. Tyranny, expressions in cruelty, and continuation of abhorrent behaviors will keep you in chains.

Those that are upon the Earth now have one of the greatest opportunities presented to an evolving civilization to advance. But it remains for you that are living now upon the Earth to see it that way. ***Seize the day then and make good!***

Where does the criminal mind begin? As we have covered in previous chapters, you have lived before, many, many lifetimes before the current one. Most of you do not know that and would find that statement not provable in terms that can be accepted in actuality or with scientific measurements that would be standards of proof. In these terms many things would not be provable. It does not mean it is not so. It means that the necessary mindset to accept, what cannot be proven, has not yet arrived within the individual experiencing the consideration on a practical level; the mindset is not open.

Many humans are afraid of other considerations that are deeply beyond known considerations. They spend a lifetime with blinders on for all areas of thought that would move them from what their minds are rigidly tied to. It is difficult to open your minds to new possibilities if you have spent a lifetime closing your minds and living in a vacuum in your regions and localities that are safe from outsiders and outside thoughts.

Many humans on the planet today, *in free societies*, live in this vacuum-like manner each and every day and will not allow themselves the freshness of free thought. Their lives are as closed books with all the pages written before their lives are over, in the physical sense. They are blocked up and unexpressive; walled off and packed up; sealed off and barely alive. Life has become drudgery at many levels, slogging day to day.

And many other people, in sharp contrast, live in countries where repression and domination are the rule, where there is no freedom, where to protest against the tyranny that is in power will cost you a life. Criminal behavior and cruelty on the part of those nations towards their populations is so ingrained in the minds of the enslaved that they, the enslaved, cannot think beyond it. It has become normalized in the mind of the subjugated. Fear keeps it, these terrible conditions of rule, in place. Tyranny reigns supreme over the millions of people that live with repression as a way of life every day.

This brings me back to the original group of questions I put forward to you in this chapter, a chapter of many considerations of what you are thinking in your heads, wandering along through your daily lives. What are you valuing? What is the purpose of your existence? I have asked you to consider much in previous chapters. I am asking much more here in this chapter as I am personally challenging all souls that read this book to rise to the consideration of who they are and what they are and where are you all going in your physical bodies? Until each soul is ready for the questions, the soul is not ready for the teachers and teachings that would supply the answers. Even so, we are very patient, as we know that these things will evolve within the hearts and minds of humankind and we will work with them through the many eons of time as we have worked with them in the past.

I said that the present civilization that is upon the Earth now, has one of the greatest opportunities to advancement and here is an example of what that might mean: An end to war, a way of sharing all resources upon the Earth. Peace that is lasting, true equality, side by side. No more need for weapons as the soul would be advanced enough to have found trust within each individual.... imagine such a time as that? A planet that is green and fresh, food for everyone that is hungry. As you could have your resources directed only at your most basic needs and there would be no need to spend the billions of dollars on defense. There would be no more need for defense because you would have given up fear, for cooperation, and through that cooperation realized a bigger and brighter world.

We say to you Earthians, these things are possible, but first you must commit to change and that is not easy. Staying within a group of thoughts that are known keeps you limited. You must get beyond your limited thought stream to get to the world that I have just described. If you only accept all things that are provable then you will not stumble upon the measures and methods of science that will unlock the new technological discoveries that will take you to other planets beyond this solar system. If your minds are only to stay within the known information, you will have no room for dreams; no room for other possibilities, and opportunities will pass you by on a daily slogging routine through lives of drudgery.

Repression, considering all of this, that has been presented here in this chapter, is a serious problem for humanity. This problem needs daily work for the proper solutions will not come easily without a firmer attunement, a reassertion of yourselves to the larger goal that drives humanity forward and upward; a goal that is a larger wish than for yourselves; a goal that is greater than something achieved for private accumulation of material wealth; a goal that is for the general healing and wellness of this great blue planet that the universe of beings calls "Earth"; a goal that is for all of humanity leading to the resourcefulness of self; self that is endless with talent and ability to render all of its problems small, especially so when working in harmony and peace with accord to the human tide that pauses only to bring in more sweetness, light, and hope, with better times forwarded and multiplying through the generations that come after what was created.

It is up to you to decide.... vacuum or freethinking? The choice is yours and so are the rewards! What are you waiting for? New doors of thought are waiting to be opened every day. This world can and will become a better place if you can *allow* yourselves the thoughts that would lead you to creating it.

This is Earth: Earth is a fabulous spaceship floating through the universe. A marvel! Oh! But this is *but ONE!* Use this magnificent "one" well and perhaps you will graduate with wisdom enough to search and soar beyond this great blue planet. Hovering through the universe is something to be dreamed of and acquiring the skill-set to make that so requires the very nature of creativity. That requires jumping ahead in your thinking and sometimes you must do that *first* in an imaginary, free spirited, uproarious, joyous way! Thereafter, you will *learn to create and give birth to your thinking*, through levelheaded processes, methodical, and rigorous, in real time, developing tangible ways to achieve the things that you have only imagined. This is the very nature of productivity, working alongside creative action through application of time, talent and inspirational thought, which refuses to give up!

That you should return to your desks in your offices and turn on your personal computers returning only to slog and then slog off to your individual nests at night retreating into more mediocrity only to return again the next day to your office desks to slog some more is a route that is below the capability of the sentient beings that exist now. You on Earth have progressed to this point. ***Now it is time to raise your heads up and turn on the brainpower that exists, in large sum!*** This requires the *belief* that you can have a better world and that you have the desire to do so not just for your material reward but also for the very privilege of making this happen.

It is a privilege to progress; to live, a privilege to lead; to pioneer, a privilege to breathe and move on this Planet Earth, which is the great home of so many eons of provable data which has led to the beings that exist now.

One does not need to review the eons of time and changes that have occurred already upon this planet and yet we say, "history should teach us to respect portability - that you take from one eon and move it into another."

Further, "That nothing that seems flat and empty really is; that the first principle is still the first principle; that you exist; that you are moving forward; that you are responsible; and that to venture beyond what and where you are now means that you must work harder to achieve!"

It is of the utmost consideration that those having the power assert their powers for the good of all. That no nation now existing on the planet is to the greater advantage of the other as the ties and points of connection currently are so entwined that great damage can be done and this is one thing to prevent-damage! As the oceans are connecting to the landmasses; the continents are connected to the water systems; the overall environment is interrelated, interconnected. There is no one waterway that does not rely on a set of codes that does not tie into the original directive set out and laid in by the Creator, long ago. Some directives cannot be changed. You must respect what cannot be changed and honor the precept - that the Creator had a reason for the basic plan.

We say again - Earthians: "a greater future *is* possible, but first you must commit to change and that is not easy. Staying in a group of thoughts that are known - keeps you limited. You must get beyond your limited thought stream to get to the greater world that I have just described. If you only accept all things that are provable then you will not stumble upon the measures and methods of science that will unlock the new technological discoveries that will take you to other planets beyond this solar system. If your minds are only to stay within the known information, you will have no room for dreams; no room for other possibilities, and opportunities will pass you by while on a daily slogging routine through lives of drudgery!"

We say again – Earthians: "Repression, considering all of this, that has been presented here in this chapter, is a serious problem for humanity. This problem needs daily work, for the proper solutions will not come easily without a firmer attunement, a reassertion of yourselves to the larger goal that drives humanity forward and upward; a goal that is a larger wish than for yourselves; a goal that is greater than something achieved for private accumulation of material wealth; a goal that is for the general healing and wellness of this great blue planet that the universe of beings calls "Earth"; a goal that is for all of humanity leading to the resourcefulness of self; self that is endless with talent and ability to render all of its problems small, especially so when working in harmony and peace with accord to the human tide that pauses only to bring in more sweetness, light, and hope, with better times forwarded and multiplying through the generations that come after what was created."

In the free societies, the world is full of creature comforts and all are spending a lifetime tied to their mental worlds within this larger physical world whirling around them. Their demands are greater than ever now to keep up with what they have created.

Yet, there is limited satisfaction, each group nudging upward towards the next level hoping to achieve some satisfaction in what is perceived as satisfaction. So many, so lost and cluttered in the daily life. It is a greater peril than you would think because this is the very mundane, boxed in, fenced-off thinking your educational societies were supposed to break you from. Yet, you are hooked in even more because of your needs, which are endlessly covetous and growing greater in magnitude.

CHAPTER NINETEEN

RESISTANCE- POLARIZATION-GETTING BEYOND OUR COMFORT ZONES

TO BEGIN WITH, *resistance to change* is something that is not easily overcome because of our conditioning to certain thoughts, which blocked us into discordant positions that remain as polarized areas. I wish to reference here, as I begin this chapter, I am assuming that not many will have the knowledge of former lives or accept the belief in reincarnation. Were the soul to come to the knowledge of having lived before, this would mitigate the following scenarios, as the soul would realize there is a connectedness to current events that have a relationship between the past lives and the present life. Let us continue on then…

Even today, as adults, we may have problems within these areas, cellular nodules created wherein trauma was experienced to the system. Given that, ageism is no barrier to hard memory logs from the past, even if subconsciously held-over childhood experiences or other stress-laden experiences of our youth, these memories have accrued.

Wherein we were on our own on the Earth plane, tasking through our daily lives, these reflected experiences collected in our minds and made life more difficult; as new injury was added to previous fractures sustained within our mental structures, furthering a pattern of deterioration.

Consciousness from within will dictate whether we surpass the red flags that stop us from moving forward to achievement or release the friction from these thoughts, which keep us as if prisoners with no remarkable reason for this hold, obvious to others or ourselves.

Requiring much… people that know and love us but, even so, the mere suggestion of change, may find us in *opposition* to what is mentioned; this feeling to oppose, to resist having started within our childhood, at the time in which teaching methods and concepts were imposed by our parents and other people in charge of our conduct and education.

We may have experienced suppression and subversion then, never truly accepting the tenets presented. *Fearing to express ourselves,* we may have been left with a worse feeling - a feeling of *inferiority* and the inability to raise our voices in contention in the arena of our life. We may have felt *powerless* to the authority above us and felt *diminished* within our own small heads, being children.

This may have caused us to doubt our own ability to think and judge for ourselves with our own gift of individual intellect. Even genius thinkers may have been limited by this early method of trouncing the young mind into the rigors of strict rules, as first and foremost in importance, even more important than the subject matter to be taught.

With intensity, even as adults, who are now free to change, long ago removed from our parents and governing institutions of learning, we will back away from changes, if these thoughts are beyond our regular mental routing, our mental daily grooves of mediocrity which have become "our nooks and crannies of everyday safety". It is not easy to impress the stronghold of the mind, to let go of the old rulebook by which it lives and governs in an "imperial fashion". It remembers the "imperial fashion" of others that struck the original grooves that we now live by.

It is not easy to proceed in the face of the battle of resistance: old areas and remnant memories of die-hards, their pain inflicted, rebirth often and die slowly. This process needs to be understood better in order to move us into the role of makers of change, as if our best friend, who loves us, is beside us talking about the immediate need to ascend, the need to overcome ourselves, take a *risk in the present moment* and move beyond *the glaring "constraints"* of our cozy comfort zones. To stay dormant in any lifetime is to miss the message completely. The message is always to move ahead and improve the world around us, as well as ourselves.

What we may not consciously know or be aware of is how our current challenges tie into the karmic lessons that we have chosen to work on in this life, choices made prior to incarnating in the current body. We will have resistance built up on record or accumulated accommodation to certain factors, certain physical points of geography on the Earth and certain personages, souls we have intertwined with in prior incarnations. These all may have underlying tie-ins to the calamities or the successes of our previous lifetimes and our current lifetime.

Suffice it to say here that the Higher-Self, however, does have the database and is the sorting mechanism of choice and will assist us as we go along in our daily activities. Nevertheless, the challenges can be tough and changing our natural alliances may not be easily accomplished. Still, we must move along one day after the other, whether slogging or soaring as an eagle! Whether pessimist or optimist, consider this: if we have reduced ourselves to average or below average achievers in life, choosing safety and obscurity rather than chance the brass rings in life which requires us to expose ourselves to risk and the possibility of failure, *then listening to even our best friend about serious change can make us cringe and pull back.*

In order to be successful in the changes we seek and wish to make, we must amend how we think, what we do, and how we motivate ourselves to go in a new direction. This requires commitment and determination, *two things that may have been watered down within us going all the way back to our early experiences with teachers, parents, and other individuals that first taught us to "give up" on ourselves;* to believe that we could not win; that our minds were of lesser intelligence than those that taught us, those that ruled with iron hands.

Creativity may have come out of us then and rooted, but it was stamped out and may have been strangled out of us by those that surrounded us and oppressed us into submission, harshly and with imperial-like authority. Encouragement from adults would have been lacking if this were the circumstance, as young fresh minds challenging authority were oftentimes not appreciated in the classroom or at home.

We may be suffering now from a lack of remembrance or appreciation for what we were routinely subjected to as children. Difficulties now with bad habits or habits of neglecting ourselves or others around us whom we love or difficulties allowing ourselves, or others, to fully flourish in whatever we choose, may be direct tie-ins to the past, a past that is limiting us now in our present choices, actions and deliberate inaction or lack of making choices to amending our conditions. This leads to lives of frustration, stress, and futility.

Observation tells us, as Spiritual teachers, that this world has too many people that have been suppressed and damaged in their early lives as children. Too many that have been abused or subjected by inference to adult circumstances. These circumstances children have become a part of due to family environments that were regularly filled with fear, emotional disturbance, and neglect. As their parents were lacking a total sense of well-being within their workplace, community, and personal relationships with marital partners and others, the children can continually suffer much like children abused through alcoholic parents; children living out their young lives as if alcoholics themselves, because of conditioning and mere presence in the lives of their addicted parents.

Unfortunately, this mindset and learned behavior can set up a series of tough negative points of reference and polarization for the children to overcome during the course of their adult lives when they are in the world and on their own completely and yet unable to detach from what was taught and experienced in a negative manner during their young lives. These pictures and feelings have been gathered in the mind and will cause disruption when other new thoughts and circumstances come into play in their lives, bearing some resemblance to the thoughts and conditions of their troubled youth pattern and causing new pain and suffering through current lost challenges and desires getting squashed on a daily basis. Repetition of circumstances seems to impress the mind that it is flawed and unable to achieve, no matter which direction it takes.

Seclusion or withdrawing from life is a clear indication that this mindset is still in place and effectively causing trouble in the present. This can create a pattern of under-achievement in life or even serious maladjustment to the demands of everyday living and supporting oneself in a sensible career producing something to sustain one's world. *Lacking confidence* to open new doors and risk experiences in the world that would represent real challenges and opportunities to grow and advance and at some point, experience abundance, would result.

These carryovers of emotional resonance would follow us into our own individual adult lives and unless we have *separated out and away from* these powerful thoughts and imposed conditioning of others, which have held us back, we are likely to be, in this present moment, *still under the influence*, although we may not recognize it as so.

Yes, we may find ourselves still influenced, even NOW, by the memories of the people from our past and thoughts projected upon us and strictly taught by others in authority from our young lives wherein *we were not in control* and then beaten down and back from developing our inner selves; *privately rich interiors waiting to be built*, building that is essential to making us happy, responsive, and productive adults.

Now here are some prime examples, indications of stumbling blocks, points of polarization that show us, even as adults, privately rich interiors *which have not been properly developed or fully furnished…YET! (As Spiritual teachers we remain hopeful, even as we are presenting this listing):* The weight problem is a good example of a case in point. We say we want to lose weight, yet we go to our regular diet, which keeps us only fat. We rest upon a couch at the end of our day exhausted and tired of the rat race. Our bodies cry out for movement, fresh air, and healthy exercise but we turn a deaf ear and seek only to be left to our regular TV show, where movement of our bodies is not required. Passive, life moves away from us and precious change seems like too much work. Optimum health passes us by, easily.

I start with that area first, as so many now need to remember what I have discussed in the previous chapters. That the purpose of food is primarily to properly nourish the body and maintain the condition of proper assimilation, restoration, and continuity of prime functionality of systems within the scope of the entire body. This body, the human body, was designed for optimum health. (Please return to our previous chapters if you need to refresh yourselves about the concept of optimum health and how to achieve it, as this has already been taken up for points of discussion in this first volume of study.)

In today's world I would stress that the food to nourish our bodies, if taken within proper portion and of proper choice, would be food to nourish our bodies and nourish our souls as well. The physical body is our vehicle to drive through life, but the soul encased within the physical body is given to us for eternal maintenance. Temporal is all food. Eternal is all Spirit.

It is a holy moment, to eat and feel the presence of food in our body of human flesh. Treat it as such and if this moment can be shared with others, by all means make life "joyful" in the receipt of food and loved ones at our table, as these are gifts furthering our very existence, as is the clear water that accompanies every meal. Water is essential as being in and of itself, prime nourishment for our total well-being.

Light candles and bring flowers and add to these tender moments of food intake. You are blessed with family and dear friends, gifts both seen and unseen. These thoughts will nourish you much beyond the expression of eating food, as one part is temporal and the other is eternally registered upon the soul. Sharing what our hands have gathered only increases the value to the Spirit, which lives forever. What we are feeding is the creation of optimum health as the soul growth is promoted and improved with new experiences that enrich our lives, again and again, time through memoriam.

Inability to use a talent is another area, often leaving the soul in a quandary as to the explanation; this quasi-like example of polarization can be well established in the mindset, early on, which then may snowball feelings and emotions into a large stumbling block, a block that needs to be removed as soon as it is recognized; yet we say we want to become an artist; yet we lack the ability to permit ourselves to create and have the experience through the years to achieve the necessary arsenal of experience required to complete the job. *Fear* waters down our desire and willpower to grow our gift! Our talent sits on a shelf unutilized or underutilized. In order to allow the gift to unfold, we must both recognize the gift and then honor it by using it.

The others, the individuals, that would come into our lives and help us harness our gift in ways that would represent materialization in dollars and cents fashion will come, but they will come about after the original gift has been accepted and practiced by the soul that brought it over from this side first, before birth. Before birth we choose the talents or main career desires that we wish to express and grow in the next life. This is how it is and the thought of honoring the gift will come back to the soul. Signaling again and again is this request and refrain, to honor the gift; this signaling process in the brain will most likely continue until the soul "gets it" and tries to make it right.

For the soul needs to develop its own sense of identity and that it does try to do within the lifetime, sometimes with success and sometimes without the hoopla of public or monetary recognition. The inner voice continues to speak until we learn to listen and gain the confidence to act. Trusting in our own "knowing" may take a lifetime to accept and grow to the point where we can see the power of this trust in action and materialization of what we want around ourselves.

Pick up a talent and use it. It is never too late! Expression of the gift honors the gift and, in another lifetime, it may become possible to grow the gift at that time if there is not the means and time to gratify oneself in that manner in the present life. Nothing is ever lost. The soul is always in growth and going forward. There is *no time to lose!* Just know that the talent is a choice and start to use it daily and the soul will then find some peace and harmony including what it instinctively knows it is to do and express. ***End the resistance.*** **Accept the gift and grow the gift**. This would reduce the point of polarization and build a positive connection to the gift. The brain center would then prosper from the additional use of creativity in this area, a creativity that is a blessing and a necessity to optimum health and a happy life wherein we live and are fulfilled with our loved ones and life agreements.

Education is another area wherein stumbling blocks can become highly charged matters; yet we say we want to go to school for higher education, yet we do nothing to start on that road or once started on the road quickly allow ourselves to fall off the road and get plowed under by routine life. We quickly make excuses for ourselves and never look back.

If a lack of discipline existed then, it would have reflected immediately as we showed up on the college campus of our choice; finding that we could not complete our studies; we could not adapt to the loneliness; we could not keep our minds on the subjects we wanted to learn. Our mood can turn somber quickly, especially if the soul thinks that the level of education would only be at the level of the demands of a high school curriculum.

If we thought we were smart in high school, now we see that we are in the room with others from many other regions of the country that have arrived with their smarts also.

True competitiveness is pressure and with a professor at the helm who is liberal or worse, who is liberal *and remote*, we have the responsibility to listen and absorb the work as presented or suffer the consequences if we are lax. The responsibility to learn is squarely on our own heads! If we have not developed a strong sense of self, we may fall by the wayside and feel inadequate against the challenge.

Alas! The demands of being interjected into a *freedom society* which may exist on the campus wherein there exists no parental support may cause some to get off track, quickly, finding that they do not manage themselves well as to time and economy of class work. Wherein no parental help is available, the soul would have to rely upon what it has developed for itself at the time of the studies. Many souls cannot get to the root of this problem. The problem is that the home environment is still affecting the child. If the home environment is not good, the child will feel this loss and not do well in the adult world, especially as he/she begins with their studies in the first year of college. If the young adult has not built its own private interior, the soul will feel it intensely missing at this time. These feelings can be harsh and overwhelming to the young mind that has not built its *own reservoir of self-confidence.*

In the first year of college we may also find that we are forced to work to put ourselves through the courses, as our circumstances do not permit us the luxury of a parental payment for our education. We may find that college loans are required and then there is pressure imposed upon the welfare of the student right from the start. The need to succeed is pressure on the shoulders of the young freshman that is trying to stay on course and balance all of it. For many young students this is truly devastating.

If depression sets in, the "wish desire" can be shut down. It is the same principle as in the matter of love. We grow cold quickly. We can quickly lose the attraction to the thing we thought we wanted most. Now it turns swiftly to disaffection…the desire to escape from the daily attendance of school or worse yet, we attend our classes but may find that we are not able to concentrate on the work as the mind has gotten so clogged with the thoughts of all the things that must go on in order to get what we thought we wanted, an education. We may drop out of college and regret it further down the road of life.

Accept the challenge. Study! If you are reading this now and this seems like your problem and circumstance of the past, it is time to return to school. Pick up the books again. Even if in the middle of our lives or nearing the end of our life, ageism is not at issue here, as education is a beautiful thing, an essential gathering for oneself, regardless of the chronological age, regardless of the starts and stops along the road to that education. Again, it is never too late! No one is to lose!

Pick up the courses and studies again and add this knowledge into your daily life. This connects us to the original challenge and removes us from creating further damage to ourselves continuing with the belief *in our lack and inability* to achieve what we most desired. Where we can win, we should. Take up the battle again! This removes a set point in the brain center and convinces us that we have the willpower to complete this mighty task, wherein we felt defeated in our youth and left out in the cold as adults.

This "comeback" establishes a sense of well-being to the overall life and we will use this experience as an example for those around us and ourselves, as to what can be accomplished *when we have created the trust and spirit for a change and the courage to start again* on that road to completion of our higher education.

The soul can then feel joy in overcoming. This is a strong building block then and nevermore a stumbling block. Victory replaces defeat and that builds self-confidence and makes possible other achievements as we move along in our lives as the mindset has been improved. Our journey becomes sweeter and made sweeter for all those around us too that have watched our makeover and may think about what they might do for themselves.

The monetary rewards achieved in this process or as a result of this process are by-products of the acquisition of the knowledge. As the knowledge is added to the brain center reservoir of study and achievement, it may be put into action in a future lifetime. We are limiting ourselves if we allow ourselves to think that *there is no time to* express our education, as in this lifetime we may be too old to find a career or a job wherein we can apply the higher education in actionable work.

Love is another area of resistance and polarization that needs immediate clarification if we are to be happier people in love relationships…yet we say we believe in love and then quickly choose what is not love, but readily available! Afraid to wait and fearing that this may be the only one that wants us, we take what is offered to have one under roof and THEN wonder why we are not happy? Loneliness breeds easy acceptance. Misery loves company.

Of all the matters to sort out, polarization points, well established in our brain centers regarding love, the giving and receiving of love, the choices of whom to love, and the ability or the lack of ability to come forward to love, are some of the most important choices to be made in our lives and yet these choices are so difficult for the soul.

If we have not studied about previous lifetimes, then we do not have the advantage of what these studies would give us regarding the soul mate and the choice of the soul mate that is made before the crossing into the new life. Then we must hope to meet our mate early in life, which is why we often choose to return to the same families and areas of geography, as it is never just about one soul, but, rather, it is about two souls, the life mate being one of the necessary parts of a full life.

But if, in our life, we met with discordant experiences, then we disconnected, in vibration, from our soul mate, our soul mate keying into that vibration and sparking acknowledgement through that vibratory process. But if that vibration has been changed because of the discordant experiences that occurred prior to meeting the soul mate, it will make recognition harder for the two souls to pick up the connectedness, the radiant signal, and feel the heat of the matching correspondences that are underlying the meeting.

But when it goes right…this is always a beautiful experience of great import when the two souls meet and spark together. To witness, for us as Spiritual teachers, is always moving and reason for Spiritual celebration on our side, as we know we have served humanity well in our mission of alignment assistance.

However, if we cannot locate the signal from our natural soul mate, life is difficult. We may have married or one part found another for a lesser mission. This is what can happen and we say that truth is the "wish desire" the heated motivation, is for the perfect one and that the soul recognizes the perfect one when that one is in front of the face. ***The wish of the soul is that the perfect one be recognized.*** – That is the message from the heart and we are wise when we are mature enough to wait for this one exclusively. But as so many do not wait, they then lack the happiness that they would have felt with that exclusive one. And therein lies the reason for so much conflict and unhappy lives as we have married the wrong one, having not developed the interior personage that would have led us naturally to the physical path crossing of the mate. This is crucial to understand, as nothing can then make up for this grand loss. The soul is looking for the "one" and the "wish desire" needs to come forward but will not express itself until the very one has crossed our path. As it is so, we are made a wiser community with love in our lives, as there is no match for a true love felt and appreciated daily. This is a joy and a blessing for a lifetime.

What to do then? Know that this is true: If you find yourself without a soul mate, it is better to live without than to manufacture something less than true love and give your life over to that. Discipline in this area is tremendous growth for the soul. If you are reading this and feel that you have never found your "one" it is wise to acknowledge that here, at this time, and then to know this and in another life we will be stronger and choose better, having gained the knowledge here, in this volume of study regarding the love mate.

In the interim, we must take up the issue *of loving ourselves* and put that love in action in acquisition of a good life for ourselves. It is not only on the monetary rewards acquired in our life that we built. Matters of finance may house the body but do not necessarily guarantee the satisfaction and joy of the heart. If you are reading this and find that you are alone and without, it is a moment to consider what you might do for yourselves to increase, now, at this very moment, provisions for yourself. *Look for a new path!* One that will bring you to loving yourself better and then loving others that enter your field, aura, making this road more blessed and joyful as you are surely upon that road now. *Seek and new doors will open unto you!*

And we say that in our life, whether we know it or not, we are making progress. Even from the greatest stumbling block that we have created in our minds, we are changing and moving to the light and this light will bring us the peace and harmony we seek. Only in accepting this truth can we ever find happiness and as Spiritual guides, we see in this world of revolutionary industry and progress, still the people are believing in so little that is love and so much that is not love and settling for lives of futility based on choices that were so low in vibratory matching. The soul needs the life partner to be within its own range of vibratory influence. Matching correspondences are so difficult and that is why we must grow stronger so that *we can attract into our lives the soul **mate that we were meant to be with.***

To wit, we say: Love is still the best! Love all that surrounds you and *believing is half the part that gets us there **but oh so great is that part!***

CHAPTER TWENTY

THE ART OF MANIFESTING WHAT WE WANT, RECOGNIZING WHO WE ARE NOW

TO BEGIN WITH, it should come as no surprise to anyone reading this, whether a believer in metaphysics or a non-believer on these subjects, that we do not always get what it is that we ask for and seek. There are very good reasons for this.

Our belief systems will oftentimes limit us in what we will allow our minds to conceive as possible. Traditionally, to believe in "lack" is what fills the mind and never leaves the orientation of the mind for many human beings around the globe.

In this chapter, I will discuss some of the thoughts that stand out in our mind file and limit our possibility for achieving and going after what we consider our wants and our needs versus our highest aspirations, bringing our dreams into reality.

What really takes place in our lives, beyond the dream state, is at another level. We will unfold more understanding on these matters in this chapter, delving into the alignments to the "what and why" of these places in our mind and how they propel and capture us in the human form translating into action or inaction, resulting in manifestation as desired, or lacking of manifestation as planned and hoped, due to our inaction or other circumstances surrounding our "wish desire".

Let me say further that I have deliberately let the matters of the mind come in at the end of this volume as many of these matters are deep, very involved, and require much thought to translate here upon the page. The human psyche is highly evolved energy!

Bearing this in mind, a strong second consideration, as to what we ask for and seek versus what we manifest in the reality of the Earth plane, is this: that sometimes the soul is not ready for the harsh realities of life, the extremes of it, the required endurance and seemingly unending "push and punch" demanded to garner what we would like to obtain.

There are no guarantees. There is no exact formulation of these matters whether on Earth or on our side in the Spirit world. There are projections, probabilities, prospects, and many road signs along the way. This is especially the case on your side, the Earth plane, the blue planet, as here we must say again that we have no human bodies to deal with and no human needs to fulfill on a daily basis, as is your case on the physical plane. There is no time clock here, in the Spirit, to keep up with. Only time era records which are referenced for overviews, used mainly as reviewing tools, when our guides work with souls, after completing each lifetime in human form.

The purpose of returning to life in the physical body is to have the sojourn that was promised, with good intentions, from here. We have explained this process in an earlier chapter.

For now, suffice it to say, that from our side it is many times *more happiness projected* than can be achieved by the soul once it reaches the Earth plane, the plane of matter, where it must demonstrate with action. Whereas, in the plane of matter we are sheathed in a human form, this is not the case in the Spiritual realm. This Spiritual realm is being experienced in total *only after* the Spiritual, elastic-like connecting line electrifying the human form, is broken, which happens at the time of death to the physical form. This line connects to both worlds.

This human form requires much to be stabilized as it is functioning in a physicality which is limited to aspects of geography, gravity, time (time which is the product of your world) and all that comes into play as the survival mode takes over. Through all of this, human passages may make us less "positive" in what we take away from it all in our thinking, our imbued feelings, our pictorial memory records, and may make us more negative, teaching us *limitation*, fear, and caution within our choices and our actions. Even so, each soul crosses to the Earth plane again with our love and best wishes for a happy and prosperous return.

On this side, the projection for the next life is made based on the decisions of what is to be accomplished, which are guided decisions from our Spiritual groups in conjunction with the advancing entity, which is going forward, returning to the plane of matter. But, once the soul is into the new Earth sojourn, we can never be sure that the soul will reach what it has projected from here.

Free Will! It is up to us to do, to choose. This is the case, whether that concerns the best wishes and intentions *for securing a true love*, or the sincere wishes for securing the intended career and the *desire to achieve in some meaningful or notable fashion*. The consequences of the life will present themselves and the Oversoul, the Higher – Self, is the guide through the daily life process. Each soul goes through this process alone and must gain control of itself during the life phases of growth to old age. Each soul rises to the individual life challenges. Our family, friends, and spouses are our companions along the path. What we do with them is our story and why we choose these relationships is also our story! All of it together becomes our template, our building map, spanning our lives and eras.

The will of manifestation is what I will discuss here, in this chapter, as this issue of manifesting is in so many respects, *the art of creating a strong will power* during the course of the life. Let me explain as we move further into this text, hopefully you will see the connection points and gain knowledge, confidence, and understanding of the mental process as it unfolds, within the life. Further inserting into your mind, the concept of achieving what you want through radiant positive energy! With your intellect, rise above all obstacles, which seem to make your thoughts of overcoming, *overwhelming!* **Rise to the challenge; get beyond your fear and over spent caution.**

The art of manifestation varies in degree, relative to the soul that is up to the task and the level of ability to project through to the manifestation of what is sought. Not all have achieved the same stamina and commitment to "stay the course" which can call upon the soul to hold on through strenuous or severe circumstances, obstacles to overcome which are required in order to achieve what is sought.

As souls will vary in age and life returns, some will have more experience coming from past lives, where wisdom was achieved. Other souls, which have not lived as many times, may be junior in trial experience and not able to manifest as well as those that, are senior upon the Earth, having been tested through many more hardships through previous lifetimes. The talent may be there in a soul but the necessary ingredients to back the talent may not have been developed, as *of yet. However, there are none to lose! Let us keep moving then…*

If you will recall, I explained why the age of the soul is so important to what is achieved in any one lifetime and why there is always a soul age mix upon the Earth. Go back and read that chapter in this volume if you need to refresh yourselves before we begin here as we have discussed so much already, sometimes in general terms, and upon other pages in very specific terms, in this, *volume one of the Rama series.*

In synopsis, the planet is never left without leadership from sage souls that must hold the basic course trends and requirements to set the pace of growth for the overall world pace. In each category, the Earth plane will have its leaders and pioneers to assure that progress will continue and the rest of humankind will come along at their own pace following and bringing up the progress of the multitude at large. This is the case through many rounds of humanity upon Earth, the blue planet.

It is my intention to dictate four books to this scribe if it would be her intention to receive them. However, this is a transmission which requires dual participation. I am not in a physical body. If this were an easy task, many souls on Planet Earth could take my *notes, but many cannot take my notes as they cannot hear me* to receive me in meditation. This is her gift. Cooperation and follow-through in the material world, Mrs. Lindsay's world, are not guaranteed. This scribe must rise and bring the words to print. Essentially, we are dwellers on two planes. I trust that Mrs. Lindsay will complete her mission. She now lives with greater purpose because of receiving this data.

I want to say here that when the soul recognizes the over- soul, the Higher - Self and is in total communion with the Oversoul, *the art of manifestation is at its highest point.* Why, you may ask? Because the Oversoul has no problem in heightening the down pouring of awareness to the soul in a concentrated manner. The Oversoul teaches the mind of the soul that it is releasing itself on a daily basis from the hold of the physical body and is in communion as much with the mental process stemming from the directed energy field of the Oversoul as the natural physiological processes of the human body.

The goals that remain for the individual that has studied and is applying the tenets taught through the metaphysical studies greatly increase the possibility that the soul will achieve much that was intended in the course of this lifespan because of this open connection which is powerful and truly remarkable. Many things that the Spiritual will provide will come through the Higher - Self without interruption or blockage simply because the entity has lit the body up with acknowledgement to the existence of the Oversoul and the connection to the Spirit world which is everlasting and truly a firm reality, both worlds having the consistency of co-realities.

Once this open "consciousness union", synergy, occurs it will make the life of the graduate of metaphysical studies wiser in all actions. The willpower will become stronger and the temptations into actions, which would lower the soul into degradation or other things, which will degrade or drop the level of the soul, this soul now will instinctively find no further interest in. Negative attractions to people, places, and things which might have caused problems before, will simply *not have the hold* over the soul as before, as the soul has located a new willpower and leaves the association of all that as distasteful.

The entity will feel the presence of the Spiritual guides, as the Spiritual guides will now honor the gradation of an ascending Spirit and help it to achieve a better life in all matters. This entity will be guided away from harm and losses in all matters. As it is essential that those that choose this open "consciousness union" connection be permitted to grow in a fashion that establishes well upon the Earth and increases the spirituality of the planet through their mere actions and presence. However, even in these matters, free will reigns. The choice to listen or not listen in the course of communication is, in the final tally, a decision made. This is always the main challenge…given any circumstance, what is your response and reaction to it? What is it that you are teaching yourself going forward?

Even the diet of the ascending Spirit will change in accordance with the spiritual increasing. Those foods, which will load the body up with heaviness and create irritations of the inner workings of the assimilation process, will not be interesting to the entity any longer. In fact, the desire will be to go to all things lighter and add more water with every meal and will amaze the person that is being lifted up. This is all part of the processing, as the health of the soul is being pulled closer to "optimum" health.

The desire to increase the physical activity through outdoor sports is also an indication of the increasing spirituality of the soul, as the soul will naturally find this more attractive now and incorporate this daily habit of exercise into its daily life style of increasing vitality and energy. With the consent of the lower self the Higher - Self will pull all of these functions and changes together. Over the course of time the person is changed and may not even be aware of the changes that have been taking place, rapidly moving *into Spirit,* towards "optimum" health.

Conditions of the wherewithal of the soul will change also. It is not unusual that the soul will move to a new location that is for the economic betterment of itself and its family. There it will find more peace, happiness and prospects for work than in the previous location. Also, the Higher - Self will be guiding it to the new people that it needs for this fulfilling part of its life and will lead these people into the life of the expressed one.

The Higher - Self will strengthen its open directives with the lower soul and respect will grow between the two. It is not unusual that the actions of the entity become more trusting and more faithful, with recognition providing the truth in these matters. As this truth is experienced in the life on a daily basis, it lays a stronger groundwork for the future days and the soul becomes stronger as the two have a "communication process" that is more amenable to both aspects.

Through these years, validation from other people is secondary to the inner truth that the soul has grown to understand and respect on a daily basis with inner activity going on throughout the day. Practice leads to confidence in the knowing in these matters. The life will change in many ways for the better.

Example…As the Higher - Self is able to instantly message to the lower self the need to stop the car, or go to a particular place at once, this will become a summoning the soul will respond to, once it learns the process of communication between the Higher - Self and the lower self. In this way the receipt of direction is fast and many times furious, the entity not knowing why, it is to do what it receives through "inner knowing" notice or feeling to do so. This can move the soul out of harm's way and also move the soul into the path of the new people it is supposed to meet.

Reasonableness will provide authenticity and the soul will not experience coercion. Mental strength will grow and the guides will assist where discretion is questioned. The soul will learn to disregard what is not genuine, hold strong, and filter out trivial noise or interference of what comes through for participation or consideration to act in any circumstance.

Mental balance is refreshed through daily meditation, daily exercise and a proper diet that is nourishing to the human being, body and soul. It is essential that the metaphysical agent learn to properly meditate, as this will bring a calming to the nervous system. There is no equal to this method of relaxation to the physical body. All that study metaphysical matters should meditate and bring proper daily balance to the physical body and mind every day.

Another great example of open communication between the Higher - Self and the lower mind is this next scenario: if a new mate is necessary due to no mate existing in the life of the ascending soul, then by all means, if the "true love wish" is put into the request file, the Oversoul will try its best to propel the new considerations into the path of its charge. However, the matching correspondences will have to be strong for this to take place, as often the other soul will not be aware of the oncoming prospective new mate. Still, the Higher - Self will work to match up with the possibility and spark a new mate consideration. Ageism is no barrier to this process.

However, there is more to this, as now the aspirant soul who is gaining spiritual growth through the metaphysical studies will find that it is not attracted easily. The reason for this is that the vibration of the soul has changed and will not match up easily with others. To study and apply metaphysical thought into your life will raise your level of wisdom. Astara-Highlands Central, beyond the Earth, waits to assist. We are unseen, many times in the background of your life, as helpers. Expect changes, as the very life of the person that learns and lives the life of the aspirant to the higher goals is ascending from matter to soul levels that are not locked in as much to the Earth's vibratory pitch.

Following this, understand, it is not just the ability to manifest the new partner on the physical plane and attract him or her to your aura that is the difficulty. It is the process that begins prior to that happening, the pull to that particular soul having found its connection prior, *on the astral plane*. These matters of the new mate are first presented on the astral plane. There the two souls will meet in their astral bodies and test each other's natural strengths and weaknesses, in Spiritual form and matter only, as they are *still connected* to their Earth bodies, which are lying in a sleeping mode upon the Earth, at the time of this meeting on the astral plane.

Each soul has a Spiritual, highly elastic-like connecting line tying into its body. This line electrifies the body at the beginning of life, as also does the three seed atoms in the body. This energy cord line is broken at death. This cord allows the soul to move from its body and project to another plane level, without physical harm and in most cases, without physical awareness that it is doing this. Adepts to the out-of-body experience have also left the body, but in the waking state, at will. Those adept souls are far and few between as this process requires a high degree of mastership and trust.

After the meeting on the astral plane, the two prospective mates, if the matching correspondences were strong, will then, on the Earth plane, find each other. A route will appear and the couple will strike up a conversation in some manner and be given the opportunity to spark each other in person. If there are not attractions that will snag the one to the other, the opportunity is lost and the two may have another go at it on the astral plane and try a second encounter in real time or forget it all together as the interest is not strong enough for a union.

Unless the two souls have mediumship talent, they will not consciously remember that they met on the astral plane, if they even know of this plane of existence, which is the plane all human beings travel to every time that they sleep at night. The soul lifts up, by extending itself automatically, through its energy cord line, to be recharged by the astral plane energy and then drops back into the body right before the awakening from the night's sleep.

The spiritual aspect is a large one for the ascending soul, as it needs its presence of soul awareness to take up the higher tasks within the Earth sojourn. It must then have a mate that is a good fit into its current life style that will not hold back the engaging Spirit from spiritual growth.

Here is where recognizing who we are will help greatly. In recognizing who we are, we will know what we can live with and what we cannot handle in our lives. Discipline has been gained and the ability to overrule oneself in favor of oneself will be done instinctively as the soul has grown and will not allow itself to be distracted into a vibration that would draw it downward. This is especially true if the sexual attraction is strong but the circumstances that surround the person who is the prospective mate are not honest, viable, healthy, and honorable from the onset. The couple's break-up will come hard and the soul will move out of the range of one that is a temptation to destructiveness, or other behavior which could be objectionable, or in some way harmful.

This is always a critical point in the life, the mate selection. Two ways to look at this are from the rear-view mirror or looking straight ahead. Which is better…to be in line for a match with someone to add into the life but who's entrance would bring with it circumstances and conditions which would not be conducive to the life overall, or to wait and stay open to a mate who would be good for oneself completely and would bring contentment in the richest part of the life, the love life. Suitability is everything and it is great wisdom to know it and then to look to what is ahead and not what is behind. The choice is for the soul to make. Loneliness need not occur if one is *in* the life and actively using one's time and efforts towards those things in the life that make one feel *full of purpose.*

In the case of a widow or widower, this is especially true as the memory of the loved one is greatly held in the mind of the spouse that remains upon the Earth plane. Oftentimes the Spirit of the deceased will come upon the remaining spouse and try to comfort that partner and this is a good thing. However, it is also wise for the bereaved to move along as soon as possible and to start again getting involved in the business of living, loving, and enjoying life on the Earth plane to the fullest. This is important as the time can be well spent in the remaining years and need not be a depression that is everlasting.

Patience is required, however! To rush on these matters of the heart could cause havoc. Delayed gratification in the matter of sexuality is best. Given the circumstances, a "time-out" in these matters is a healthy down time. Then the remaining partner without a spouse will heal and think through the matter of mating again with a full presence of mind and emotion having gone through the grieving process alone and the adjustment to being single.

The truth is that we are all going to expire if we are in a human body. It is what we do while in the human body that is the important thing. Think of it this way…who are you? Time to look back and reflect on who you were as a child and then as an adolescent in school, to a college student, to a young person gaining full responsibility for the first time on your own, to the choice of a marital partner, to the receipt of that partner and then the prospect and receipt of a family life and on and on and on it goes. Now you are the sum total of all of it! Look at the marvel of so many turns along the road. How many times were you inconsequential to others? So many times, we do not give ourselves credit for the good deeds and good character influence we have had on others as well as ourselves. It is human nature to underrate what we have achieved. It is human to fail. It is human to count our failures first. And to remember first our experiences with tragedy and not focus enough on the *joy that was in our lives.*

If you are reading this and you have a mate, blessed is this moment as our scribe today has lost her mate and greatly loved was, he. She longs for another mate and so far, has not found one that is right for her. Yet we will continue to help her find her new mate. She has chosen to look straight ahead and not bring into her life what she cannot handle.

If we are gifted with this maturity of soul, the value of what we will add at this point in our lives has far impressed upon the soul the need for this choice of the mate to be right. Instinct is strong here and so is the willpower. To face all obstacles alone and it is alone that she takes my thoughts this day; this is her choice.

In the meanwhile, there is the teaching text that we are about to finish and it is a strong display of what can be accomplished if the willpower exists on both sides. This translation is about trust. There is trust on both sides. It cannot be created on the pages without trust.

Trust requires an honest investment of our time and our effort. If we want something to come about, *we must stay the course* with it. **Whether a book, or movie script, or stage performance, or cookie cutter magic in our kitchens to turn into a business enterprise and become famous, it is the same principal that we must believe in ourselves and then we must follow through**. The art of manifestation is the art of believing and not letting anyone tell you otherwise. It is the art of investing in us. It is the willpower to blast through the hardships along the road to develop what it is that we want. It is the redefining of what we want and remaking ourselves through our mission to the doorway of opportunity and success. It is on the go and going forward always with our confidence and trust *and not letting fear shut us down or away from our need to create.*

This is the answer for all. You can have what you want but never think it comes easily or your mission will be short lived. Oftentimes the art of manifestation is years in the making! Years! Those that would only want their "wish desire" granted in instant gratification will be greatly disappointed.

How many people do you know that have made it in the plane of matter...overnight, without struggle, pain, and many hard trials to their pinnacle? This is the message loud and clear. Trust and believe. Whether in the seeking of a lovely mate to have and to hold or the seeking of a wonderful career or the desire to have a better life for yourself and your family fulfilled - *never quit!* Never give up! Always stay positive for those who can't stay positive - will learn that success for them will be many times limited.

You can have more, if and when you believe in more. Believe, and then get going in the direction that will produce what is required within yourself to accomplish what you desire.

Go now and remember that **a strong will is grown daily.** Believing is all in casting your dreams out into the field of life! Smile your way! Hug trees and dogs on a daily basis! *There's the spirit*...good luck in making your dreams come true!

CHAPTER TWENTY-ONE

REMAINING POSITIVE IN A NEGATIVE WORLD – THE WILL TO HAPPINESS

TO BEGIN WITH, the will to happiness is within the will to survive. Happiness is the highest benefit of a civilized world; functioning often at a lofty level of existence within the advantaged world of today. Law and order is well established upon the Earth in these areas and we have written about this within our text already, as well as having discussions, in depth, regarding communication modes, which have made the rapid exchange of visual, audible, and print text information possible to many parts of the world concurrently.

But whose world is it? A tricky question, as it seems that there are worlds within worlds, within still other worlds; worlds of our parents, worlds of our grandparents, and worlds studied from histories of people and animals upon the Earth from prehistoric times; worlds so ancient that we can only imagine them as they are cited in a book and imagined in our minds.

Spatial latitudes, well established in our brains, can make heaven or hell for us, while in the human body. Literally or figuratively, it is the human brain that is at work, and this system is complex, having been developed over eons of time, much beyond the one day of creation theology rule so set in the minds of many upon the Earth.

You will recall that in previous chapters we discussed the matter of what we manifest, this being a function of and about what we are thinking. You will recall, also, that I said "that nothing stays flat, that all is in motion through a progression, whether it is understood or not, this is still the case; that all things are in progression and are not static in the least; that there is a plan in motion too and that the entire plan is not understood yet by humanity." This is deliberately so, as the Creator has seen to it. This design is in motion today and will guide the worlds through to their next levels of ascendancy.

All things are in spatial latitude and in coordination with each other. The universe is not without guidance from the Supreme Being and this leadership is infinite, set in motion by the Creator from the beginning of infinity, of which we say that moment is not known. Only the Creator has the knowledge of the commencement of infinity and we should begin to see the light in these truths as we move from the mid-point of development of the blue planet and move into the next motion, which will be a guided exploration of space. Minerals, materials, and understandings of this travel mode will come of age and discernment by the human beings in progress there, upon the Earth today.

Spatial latitudes exist for all things and peoples of the universe. There is a rhythm and rhyme to all of it! Each pattern is designed to stay within the zones and boundaries of that existence for proper and best coordination of life. Gravity can be manipulated and those that know how to do so are in the air today exploring other planets. But your planet, the blue planet, has not progressed to that level and we will talk about the universe in our next book, but for now we return to the dissertation and in-depth discussion at hand which is the all-encompassing areas of the environments of Earth, in a plain, direct manner of speaking, *today's world*.

Much now, in this current lifetime, depends on the forefronts that are already established in our systems, which are fully functioning with or without us being aware that they are. Therefore, it is an art to get motivated, move into raw action and *successfully maneuver beyond* our already well-established, personal, mapped-out corners and horizons of spatial latitudes.

The human being is a relationship-oriented creature. Eons of time humans have moved from chemical formation into environments best suited for their future progression. This progression has been guided from the start, as this is not the first planet under the plan of creation and is not the last one. These are the guides that set it all in motion beyond the raw directive and material substances that the Creator has left us to work with, to use in tasking out His directives.

There is an order of magnitude, so far in advance of this order, that it is more breathtaking than I could put into words today, here on this page, to describe it. Suffice it to say that we cannot begin to tell you all of it now, there, on Earth, but to say also that you are not alone and that you will never be alone on any planet, this one or any other. Some of you suspect that now, which is a truth in terms of discovery to come about. You are now coming of age wherein this knowledge is to come to your planet and to be utilized, as the tasks and requirements in the years ahead will go far beyond any concept of life as it is understood or lived today. The spatial latitudes of today will not be the ones that will exist tomorrow, as there will be many changes, as change is the order of the magnitude of progression.

Spatial latitudes are the normalization of areas in our life style and methodology that allows us to roam freely within the known boundaries already established by us and for us through our life coordination, past and present. These areas are all encompassing, mental, physical, spiritual, axiomatic or nonlinear. This chapter will deal with our environments, friendly and otherwise - the way we view them *is key*.

Crucial to our success in life will be what our mind's governor will allow us to map out *beyond* our existing paradigms. Paradigms, aggregated dimensions and considerations, are already set-up in our mind from many previous lifetimes as to what will be our understandings from the smallest intelligence gathering range to the largest scope of widest breadth and depth of the knowledge we might possibly gain in the current lifetime.

This information will be accepted and then accelerated in our brain system, first coming through as a reflection of previous data already collected by the brain center and carried over into the current life stream. The souls that have gathered knowledge in these intellectual pursuits prior to the current lifetime will, most definitely, acquire new information in a more positive vein in their areas of *already established* expertise. This makes the paradigms of understandings, the fully established ranges, easier for them to experiment with, pushing and expanding their knowledge basis beyond the mediocrity of others in the same field. All discoveries come first to the challenger who knocks at the door and persists that the door be opened unto him!

For instance, the man or woman who has already established well in the field of science, who in this lifetime is pursuing further the field of science, will come to the new information quickly, absorb it, and then pass by others in the field, maybe even achieving new breakthroughs within the field because the environment for this one will be *friendly. Friendly, in this instance*, with respect to this particular soul's aggregated brain center, is the established mental and physical environment of cause and action.

Friendly also means the soul's natural leaning will be drawn, will gravitate towards, the exact area of pursuit it practiced in the previous lives, prior to the current lifetime.

However, if the student that wishes to make entry into the field of science was previously an artist and has no experience in using the brain in an intellectual pursuit of science, then the experience and demands to the brain will be much more difficult.

It might have been the choice from the soul, centering on a new area to be developed, but regardless of that reason, the first pursuit and entry into the forefront of science is usually grueling and demanding, if not many times a frustrating experience for the novice student. This is because of the lack of previous range of study, experience and behavior in the current chosen discipline, which is one the brain has not acquired information on in previous lifetimes. This makes a student's choice of career in that area more difficult as it is in the very beginning of acquisition of data required to grow in the new area or field of endeavor.

As we have already stated in prior chapters, the brain center, which center is gathered and increased upon from lifetime to lifetime, is running in an aggregation mode. What we build upon today, if we achieve well in that area, has probably been an area that we have practiced into perfection in previous lifetimes and should not be viewed with an eye towards mystery for explanation or proof positive of current "genius". There is no magic in what I am saying. Pause and think about it. The lifetimes are not run in isolation; there is connectivity in all we do. People, places and things will fall into various ranges as we approach them in our lives. There is no limitation to the range of development except as we would interpret through our human senses. The soul has chosen the courses it wants to develop in the current lifetime. The trouble is in not understanding that previous lifetimes existed and then rushing into things in an emotional manner, many times to the negative bent, because of the build-up of fear, "time and imposed limits" by the brain in viewing the momentary existence as a permanent manifestation. There is no room for the consideration of extrapolation of the facts, as to begin with, the facts are not fully known to lend to extrapolation. Likewise, interpolation, from Point A to Point B, in order to realize a differential, will relate to one lifetime and serve only to permit the mind to consider what is known in the current life.

Limitation to our thinking, barriers from previous lifetimes, held over infinitum, remains to our new environment, "the challenge". The challenge is always therein, to go beyond what is already known in the world and exists to tell us that these things are so, *written in stone.* But the best and the brightest have also come back in the face of these "dogmatic" throes and replied… "NO! Let us consider again the premise for the maxim…the premise for the equation, the methods and scales of our resources, to observe the observable above and beyond our known levels and horizons that exist." The true test of a scholar is not to know, but to accept *that we do not know everything. That everything is on the table for re-examination.* Not to see it that way leaves us in the abyss. This, then, is the task: to rise…to serve…to begin again and penetrate upon what is solid matter and what is not. Discovery of self is never ending and the universe that surrounds this planet is waiting to abide with open arms for those that will have eyes to see and those that have the sense of appreciation of this amazing universe; so incredible and waiting to be explored.

The human being is but another universe, equally amazing, equally incredible! We need to capture the marvel in it all. To appreciate the tremendous potential of human life and to know that we are all …pioneers! Moving across the gulf of time, traveling to a furthering of us, to the inner knowing of "us" on many levels and layers of existence and our ties to all else in our universe!

Discipline and attitude acquired on this journey through our gulf in time will make all the difference to any environment we may roam and grow into. Friendly or unfriendly, the magnitude of discussion and thoughtful consideration will bring the student to the rule of engagement. The first rule is that we must take action. To engage we must put our minds and intelligence to work. The magic is in getting going and staying the course. The science of it is ours to discover!

Discovery of "who we are now" will manifest as we grab onto the link that is our choice. There is the key. To manifest we must connect. Until we connect with it, that which drives us, we will suffer, as the choice of the soul was made prior to the current lifetime and wants to be established. This drive will continue to compel us throughout our current lifetime until we meet with it. This is the will to happiness… to manifest! Meet with "it", please meet with "it"! *We are not all directed to the same energy fields in life.* But all the fields have purpose! What is our purpose? What are our gifts to bring, to yield golden? Which field of endeavor is ours to embrace? We have all chosen various paths to take and grow upon. It is the "human will" that must work out its directives into solid consequences, actions, and manifestations.

We must learn to *appreciate the raw drive and connect to it* and then we will resolve our conflicts therein. Give way to that which would have us serve and we will find happiness in that desire. But, until we allow ourselves to have the experience, we will continue to suffer. A calling is something we must answerback to if we are to rise and follow our dream of becoming, making reality from our imaginings. The journey to "it" is our choice. Embrace your gifts and turn them into action.

We must prevail in these matters or we run the risk of repeating former lifetimes wherein we did *not rise and consequentially the negativity of our* immediacies took the upper hand. So here we are again. Will we rise or will we fall? This is not about "how much talent we have" this is about how much we will honor the consciousness from within, and allow ourselves to take charge of our lives, move ourselves into position, gain solid footing, solid standing and then create solid baselines, which will allow us to grow further and nurture our gifts and share what we have gained.

In this world, the world you are currently experiencing, there exists greater degrees of sophistication in all things, than existed in prior periods of time and yet *it feels for so many* only to complicate further the matter of *fulfillment.* That is because there are now so many interruptions to our lives, so many daily demands. Inundation and multi-tasking are the rules and not the exceptions for so many!

Penetration or concentration is for so many souls now a very difficult thing to maintain. The human mind needs to develop. It cannot develop properly without being trained to focus seriously with endurance, singularity, and proper balance. Working up to marvel creates the miracle. We become! Teaching ourselves to stay on the path leads always, *always* back to ourselves; once we have broken through our resistance, our inhibitions, fears, and polarization points that would tell us not to go further, we will start to allow ourselves to reach for the tools, the studies, and the proper experiences that would then garner for us the possibilities of creating true accomplishment in our chosen area of discipline. We become years in the making of ourselves. – We accumulate years in becoming ourselves!

For this, discipline requires acknowledgement. In a world that would teach us to "hold back" and not to expose ourselves to risk, we would learn to succumb and would not be happy, as that part of ourselves seeking free expression gets trampled upon. This is why, if we are to persist, we must learn to function "positively" in any *unfriendly* environment, facing the negatives which may be more real to us than any positive goal we have set for ourselves. Where does it exist? Within us! We are the many worlds, we are the many thoughts, and we are the many!

In a negative world people, places, and things can seem best organized and held in balance in our minds, and in check in our realities. Our responses can seem best - muted, while trying to find the appropriate responses to our proceedings. Fear can set in and trim us back and leave us with nothing. Instead of doing something, we retreat! But, if we are to achieve, we must develop that same sense of character as our predecessors. In the face of our immediate struggles and battles royal, we must be strong in order to prevail. ***Our need and sense of survival must be dominant.***

Positive energy must rise and overcome all the negatives that would keep us out of the race, keep us out of the battle, keep us sitting on the sidelines, never participating, always belaboring what we might do, what we might say, what we might conceive and keeping us immobile, *pondering only*. Positive energy is radiant currents that can electrify our minds and create with it *willpower* and an ardent determination that will take us higher with our goals and achievement. It takes courage to live! Without it we will cower and remain lost! It is the art of manifesting throughout a lifetime. Positive energy will bring us to our happiness. Contentment comes to those who persist! Never give up! Never! Any setback must be conquered or we can and will remain the vanquished!

In this technological age, the age of reason is enhanced. All of the fields of study and endeavor are heightened here, with the entire human race upon the blue planet trying to grow, learn, and improve upon what basics have already been established.

In previous chapters we have discussed at length and in great depth about the new age and the mastery of terms and understandings that are cosmic. Universality of considerations is gained through further study in the field of metaphysics. These wisdom gaining thoughts bring the student through the understandings of the universe and to the role of the ongoing developing soul which journeys throughout the lifetimes in order to achieve mastery at the end of this accomplishment. Then, there are other choices for the soul at that point of completion.

There is nothing that can explain this achievement of graduation upwards in gaining spirituality, as well as, simply studying and applying what you will learn into your daily life. Then, be guided by what you are teaching yourself every day. There is nothing to lose. It takes time to finish and gain knowledge in these matters. However, what is studied and started in this lifetime will be added to the soul's wisdom bank and carried forward into future lifetimes. It is never our goal as teachers and helpers of humanity to rush an aspirant's achievement ahead of its time. "When the student is ready, the teacher will appear". This has been a solid metaphysical adage for centuries and still holds true today.

A current religion should not be an obstacle to study – in the field of metaphysics as these studies are beyond secular teachings that are on the Earth now. The church that the student maintains a relationship with is an individual choice. From this perspective, as I have written already in the text, the student has chosen to study. Studies of both considerations can be accomplished *simultaneously* and the soul will grow as it matures in these understandings, which will result in wisdom as the lifetime continues into old age and prosperity of circumstances in the life improve.

Know, to the world at large: There is God and there is the Son of God, Jesus, which name is sacred and held in high esteem. The Spirit of Jesus is upon the Earth and the Earth will receive *forever* the blessings that His presence has brought to the planet. Further, there will always be holy ones to walk the Earth as a continuing line of good exists and will prevail, as the desire to be as He was is for many an unending vocation and drive to spirituality.

Know also: that the spirituality of mankind is being increased here, at this stage upon the Earth. This is the time when the desire will grow stronger in the human heart to connect to the presage; connecting to the Almighty. This is the time when the religions that are on the Earth will look to consolidate their positions into more of a universality theme with the force and momentum moving to the side of *good will for all men* and promotion of pursuing actions that will lead to more good will, good action, and consequence of action, expanding globally. NO corner of the Earth will be left untouched or unmoved *by this Spirit, who wishes us to be inspired to create healing of old wounds.*

It is the human heart of mankind that must learn to open the doorways to freedom and democracy upon the planet. Those countries that are experiencing communism will be difficult, as they have always been difficult because they do not want to share power. The power grabbing of the religious wars here, on Earth, which still continue upon the Earth, must end, if true liberty for all is to be achieved.

The will to happiness will grow as the heart of mankind lifts up and finds itself, self-desiring, more of a spiritual link to the Creator. This is happening now on the Earth plane. Look and you will see that the times are changing as we are writing. And the world is becoming in all matters, global. There is a global reach and consequences of actions and reactions as never before. All countries are learning quickly that they must be working in conjunction with each other or suffer the consequences of not doing so.

But the raw energy of the human race must first reach for the link to the willpower and desire to come to this marvelous existence… a world wherein *tyranny will not be allowed to exist*. This will take time, as the powers to be in so many regions of the world are not convinced it, tyranny, must change. Again, to rule as a tyrant is a great power to give up, especially when the giving up is to be done by the privileged few to the benefit of the many; the many which have been viewed only as a mass to be subjugated, a mass of people to punish and hold into submission, forever!

We, as guides, are working with so many around the globe to try and open the minds of all those in power, towards universality and good will for all. We are trying to help in every way that we, as teachers, know to help. The advancement of this civilization must be led towards the "will to happiness". This will is a wish for the *entire* human race, to the exclusion of none, to share all that it might acquire and the promise of good will and good circumstance for itself must always prevail as possibilities for the *entire globe, for all humans everywhere* that would want to achieve it as their own. **In the end, the will to happiness is the will to survive and to continue.** Astara-Highlands Central, as we are beyond Planet Earth, wishes to say: YOU CAN DO IT! Prevailing with this thought in motion … "Good will for all of mankind!" Hold this thought closest to your heart, always!

CHAPTER TWENTY-TWO

DECLINING OUR INVITATIONS TO GREATNESS, OR, ACCEPTING THE NATURE OF RISK

WHEREAS, IN THE BEGINNING OF TIME … the great

Creator stood, unlimited, at the absolute, at the edge of all possibilities, as Creation was from His hand. Into the void of nothingness, He chose and then created. He sent his courier angels to continue on with the creative chaos that is necessary to create a great parallel universe, wherein many societies could be raised up and the knowledge for the worlds pulled and rendered onto them. So mote it be!

We continue with the great Spirit to drive behind His word, His work and proceed with goodwill for all of mankind, which is still receiving the benefits of the grand mandate, the first given by the Creator to build worlds and honor Him in these worlds and to choose His invitation to greatness of belief in Him, and then become as He was. Coming to this knowledge, humanity would know and accept that God would give "all" if mankind would simply listen closely and then follow with majestic trust, *His* plan, bringing to reality *His* greatness, defined as happiness for *His* worlds.

But mankind has been stubborn and found *not* following God's dictates easily and has fled from His care which was and is still supreme, choosing instead to find their own way, which is a way with human limitation. This is still the challenge for this world today and will be until unity with Him is felt and expressed in all areas of life and walks of life for humanity around this globe, the globe called Earth, the blue planet. The challenge is to ascend spiritually and not devolve, suffering from backward movement into human flesh and animalistic behaviors that keep humanity in chains to insignificance and cuffed to the rush and pull of immediate urges for gratification in base matters.

And so, it was! However, from the beginning of time, these efforts in all matters of Creation were never easy to translate for the recipients of the information. From time immemorial, the challenge for the messenger, the one that hears, is to hear us, who are the guides and Spiritual guardians of humanity and receive the message exactly right. This is still the immediate challenge today. It takes courage to follow through!

These co-ordinations of polarities are very specific, technical, art forms and have graduated through humanity. Progress through the eons! From the very start of Creation, we have been put in place in a universal manner and have the understanding from the Creator to fulfill this mandate. We did not create this mandate. This mandate is from the origin. In order to protect humanity, we stand through the ages to keep them on the purest track over the course of civilizations. This is to assure pure progress with ethical purpose.

We are usually unseen and that also is the design. Some mediums can see us. Very few can hear us verbatim. We are at large and constantly working with each soul that is on the planet. There is no soul that is not given proper attention and full guidance. The trouble is in reception on the part of the souls and their choices are governed with free will.

Each soul was gifted from the start with his own inner voice, his own inner communication system, his own inner receiver and sender capabilities, which are innate. From what has already been written in this first book from the Rama series, you that have been reading know that I am referring to the "HIGHER-SELF" capabilities. It is important to recognize here again, in this book, that this existence of the Higher-Self has never been widely accepted by humanity, having more of a following in the Eastern cultures in many ways, than in the Western cultures and considerations. This split is not by accident, considering the circumstances and finding the world to profit from, many times over, the juxtaposition of the cultures and civilizations on the Earth, which are living simultaneously, though differently. Contrast can work effectively.

Over the course of time, however, most choose to *not acknowledge*, let alone accept and then access their own intrinsic capabilities and these elite prescient talents then remained dormant, latent in the system. The reason for this choice, to not accept their gifts, has also been presented in one of the preceding chapters, leading up to this final dissertation.

If, however, during the course of the lifetime, the person comes across the studies of one of the brotherhood groups that are on the Planet Earth at this time, then, they may or *may NOT* choose to openly connect again with themselves in a way that was never fully understood or appreciated at the start, let alone developed, overtly, into ESP (extra sensory perception) or other psychic gifts.

This is the time upon the Earth, when more are in denial of themselves, holistically speaking, than ever before. The odds are not good for so many that choose, even now, the various roads and **individual paths of inner destruction** instead of the bright light roads to ascendancy into meaningful spiritual growth.

Let us consider these various roads: These roads of destruction are full of dark images and chaos, which the brain was never created to defend itself against; as these substances were first created, inspired and brought forward for the betterment of man and then mistranslated into multi-purposes NOT intended from the start. As we have said in this book, we cannot always predict the outcome, we can only go forward with what we know to be true to the progress of man and release this information to your side when the time is best suited for the thing(s) or methodology, basic genesis of the thing, or invention or solution etc. to go forward to the Earth. But, the free will of man must take it from there. The Earth must pick up what was sent and generate the products, bringing them forward to the masses. If the translators of what was sent diminish the gifts into destructiveness, we cannot stop that process. However, there would be Karma for what has proceeded, as there is the creation of what *is good* and the possibility for the creation of *what is not good. Mankind must make the choice! We hope you choose wisely!*

Destructive roads to be aware of are as follows: Personal drugs, used for recreation, to create brain ecstasy states such as through the use of cocaine, heroin and other narcotic-like substances which affect the brain as stimulants, or put the brain into trance modes and projection into deeper regions of the brain producing holistic nightmares and pain to reflexive actions in the body; when the drug is no longer given to the brain, seizure activity is created, further pain and eventually death if the addicted are left unattended by medical practitioners. Drugs, abuse, slavery, gambling, gluttony, alcoholism, sexual depravity and addictions to sex, preservation of power, personal and national at the mercy of tyranny towards the many that must serve the mighty that prevail with force…we are not limiting the list to these destructive habits mentioned in the previous sentence, as this list could be greatly expanded if the comparison to what was granted initially to the human soul was fully grasped, which we say *it never was!*

Still, as guides and guardians to the souls, we remain hopeful that humanity will pick up the initial challenges and invitations to greatness and prevail, sharing all that is gained within the human Spirit upon the Earth, within any given era into which they evolve. We are never short-term investors, running credit default swaps, measures, means and methods of Wall Street! Truly, M O N E Y is mania to so many in your world. Perhaps, it would be wiser to not abuse ourselves with our means and circumstances. There is much wisdom to be gained from having and wanting less of things and then **focusing on what has already been given**!!!! Some things are material and truly mortal, other things are for always possessing in themselves the potential for eternal life; Gratitude for one and appreciation for another. Denial *will keep us weak and wanting.*

Think about it like this…truly…is the glass half full or is the glass half empty? A point of meditation no matter what circumstance upon the Earth we find our current selves, in and about. Where does lasting evaluations and valuation of existence exist? Whose rules make it so? What is truly of value? What is lasting? Where is the gold of the everlasting? What is the true quest? Where is happiness? Where is the soul in the midst of this mystery that is the journey through life and to life?

The obsessive attraction to things and the collection of things and creation of empires that repeat the mistakes of the past, for many souls, is an obsessive lesson that all must graduate beyond. For surely, we say again, the soul is eternal and it survives the physical world, any physical world and any particular lifetime, to emerge as much more than the ever-translucent traveler between worlds and lifetimes. The soul is ever-reaching and everlasting through this entire experience in and out of the human body and that is the fact in motion as we write herein.

The main struggle upon the Earth for so many is the initial one, to move beyond what can be gained through material acquisition, which is not always satisfying, so much so, that many souls can never find happiness. They miss the message altogether-and cannot see the forest for the trees; the soul, its pure existence and the possibilities of what that gives to humanity, which at this time remain completely underrated.

The inner whisperings of the soul, *so suppressed* in humanity, will give the Spirit a hard time rising above it all to equalize with the human body and the mind it was meant to master. Mastership becomes almost impossible, leading to the furtherance of many more lifetimes repeating unhappiness, as the soul cannot find what it wants. It is never satisfied with what it has. The soul creates lack luster life; we say, life without the most valuable ingredient, the full expression of love and sharing. The souls in this world move along with differences and complaints expressed and create a very hard time and rigid environment integrating with others and a culture beyond the one it is raised in, exclusively.

Even today with civilization, wherein worldwide communication is possible, the soul is not translating at the high velocity which comes through applied study, meditation and letting the Higher-Self govern and open its soul which is encased and imbued with a full mission to ascendancy and growth of the Spirit to widen during the presence of itself and application of "goodwill" in the immediate lifetime.

This explains further the sometimes-perplexing truth of the following facts: the quality of life here on the planet is still in many countries utterly deplorable and the western worlds that have advanced, view it only in the context of distance, sitting safely in front of their television sets, viewing with objectivity and ofttimes indifference. Many "just watch" the other parts of the world in utter consequences and give in a charitable way, a money donation. But these that gather to watch *do not feel* that it, these utter conditions in other parts of the world, are things that they *can really change* or have the responsibility to change. A safe disconnection is created, consciously or subconsciously, which allows daily life to continue uninterrupted. These "other" issues are left to the political fronts that sanction the world.

With diplomatic accords here and there, politicians view world conditions, *again* with a dispassionate sense and disconnect to the other problem areas and underdeveloped situations on the planet when it is about selective "interest" to the individual countries, such as the United States. These matters present again to the international groups such as the United Nations, *wherein again,* "selective interest and dominance prevail".

However, God will always have his warriors, his patriots. **What is the invitation to greatness? It is the invitation to the truth revealed within us.** It is the invitation to be as He was. How is this possible you may ask? The "man on the cross" did not ask for fortunes upon the Earth. He spoke of a kingdom that was more of heaven than Earth. He asked all to connect to Him and to follow Him with love. He asked the people to love as he loved and love well, sincerely and to be devoted to others. He taught that the face of one was the face of the many and to help one was to connect to all and in this way are we made great, are we made whole.

189

There is no higher message than the message of "LOVE" and yet still that message is not heard, is not lived. The one named, Jesus, Son of God, came upon the Earth to personally deliver this message. In human form He lived and died. Divinity scourged and then crushed onto a cross!

Saviors or mediums, are they raised up? From the beginning of time, the two worlds have used and abused their messengers and the messengers themselves have never had an easy road as it is an unparalleled challenge for most to hear, decipher and then translate to the text what is heard in the human mind and then given to be correct for the benefit and welfare of the human strain, humanity, which is on the Earth at the time of the medium's existence.

The second message from Jesus was one of Brotherhood and what we might achieve if we lived as He lived and loved as He loved over the course of our lifetimes. It was a message to spend broadly across the universe upon all who are residents of the world that is Earth. It was a trial period for Jesus taking on the human form and raising it up with mastership through Spirituality. His lesson, though, was larger than that. The lesson has been missed by many to fully accept that *we could also* perform miracles and do all of the things that He did, meaning we would have to believe as He believed, then act.

If you look around the world and read through the histories of the World, some great saints have lived upon the Earth and taken up the cross as He did and truly developed as He did in the human form but kept it clothed in a growing divinity, growing always until the human form was graduated and given up. This message is the larger one for the world to accept…to be as He was, yet it is easier to pass that message by as it is so difficult for many to live the message and accept that in recognizing that this could be so, means we would have to become, to do something about our potential.

The invitation to greatness is always at hand. *It is this one…and there is no greater messenger and teacher of these higher lessons than Jesus. The Earth is forever blessed with an Almighty Spirit as large as this Master, the Master Jesus.*

Now, the nature of the risk to rise has always been great as the societies that the medium existed in were always troublesome for a "prophet", society not accepting the talent that is the medium, or worse, even a King serving the head of a prophet up on a silver platter to a King's paramour in payment for lust! Whether a King or general populace, it was *the independent Spirit* of the prophet that came through, which so rocked and rallied the world! The Spirit collective from the other side, the side that beckons us home after the Earthly sojourn, is a warrior Spirit, crying out in any wilderness, along the journey to and from these worlds, a journey we all do partake in, say we.

But many have accepted the invitation to greatness as writers have filled the books with text, but no writer so great as to fully capture the very nature of God! Forever being rewritten, are the understandings of God, as his creators perceive him and get to know him over eons of time. The truth is revealed! GOD LOVES US! That this story continues is the very essence of His essence, as we cannot go forward with yesterday's misinterpretations and misunderstandings gleaned from the old times.

God is great. God is eternal. The Godhead is at the core of infinity. All that derives comes from His beginning. We do not exist without His future and the future does not exist without His past and all of these things are from the Creator, gifts for humanity! So splendid is His great plan for the worlds and the citizen souls.

Humanity suffers from a deep lack of trust. If all could trust, greater progress could be made upon the Earth and the things that need to change conditions upon the blue planet would come about much easier. Races would be more cooperative if they could perceive that the message of Love was the true first principal and that all other goodwill comes about through following the first message. Integral to that message is the message of freedom. The freedom of the souls therein is the commitment to allow the societies in the worlds to uphold the principals of freedom first. The Earth could then become a paradise much more so than it is today.

Humanity suffers now from the lack of trust and lack of belief that the Creator is the beginning and that His beginning was no mistake and that we must trust in Him above all else and listen to what he would task us to do in our lives. A desire to connect to Him would bring us closer to ourselves than ever before and we would find an internal happiness that only a saint could explain and then not nearly as deep as when felt one to one. Each soul was meant to experience this total reflection of God and gain His countenance by the end of a lifetime, any lifetime. This is the mission. Let us begin again to consider this mission, this journey of the life we live within the body that is us, NOW!

The Creator's genius is matchless by any one human or group of human beings coming together to think, greater than any creations that they come together to improve their world with; none of these, SUPRA, outdo, the Creator as His wisdom and intelligence are consummate in the Universe of all universes.

He is the First of all-firsts. That his co-creators, who create in the worlds and on the planets, such as the people of Earth, do not understand is at the core of the problem. Yet, **He extends constantly the opportunity to accept His invitation to greatness**, an invitation that each soul has and many times does not understand. When in some fashion a glimmer of it is understood, even then, it is declined.

It takes great strength and courage to become wise and follow Him! The human Spirit is reluctant to grow wiser, taking the easier roads instead, where less is required and ignorance is bliss! There shall be trust and putting our feet on the path to follow what it is we believe and letting nothing deter us from our mission which is central to getting there, isn't it?

Do you think it is far easier to live through many lifetimes as opposed to one lifetime to come to this wisdom? But then, as most do not believe in many lifetimes, they do not view this as a real choice, just as they do not view the consideration of being like Jesus, a real and tangible choice either, while in the human body.

SUPRA is at the level of the Creator. Those that succeed greatly upon the Earth have been annoyed with the mediocrity of life and then gone off on their own to identify one area of consciousness wherein they can express themselves in concentrated effort over the course of the lifetime. These are the developers and focused groups upon the pages of histories and these are the ones *that have taken just a sliver of the truth of the vast and broad invitation to greatness and then applied themselves*. This invitation to success is both spiritual and practical. A genius expressed in producing an abundant stroke of materialism is simply another way of accepting his gift; co-creation is always best when it is applied genius. It is the developed belief systems of these individuals in the one area of focus in their lives that attracted them and kept them glued to that area of consciousness for a lifetime. These people were pulled as if by a magnet to their causes; and courses of action in their lives always got help from this side. NO soul is upon the Earth without Spiritual help and companions along the path. Recognized or unrecognized, we are there in the background.

But everyone has an invitation to greatness; the simplest, poorest human is not banned from this invitation, as the invitation is innately burned deeply into the soul from the very start, from the very first incarnation. But so, few understand this and continue without grasping who they really are and how much potential they truly have to take- up in the life.

To begin with, no soul is really poor. This is to miss the point entirely as each soul has been enriched with the Spirit Center that *is* the Creator. Take up your cross then and move along. Readers of this text were drawn to this moment. It is your moment. What do you want? Time to see things differently? Perhaps you will become wise. You must choose and you must do the doing. We are not human now- we are Spiritual guides. Many of us have graduated long ago and some of us never experienced human life at all, but exist in other forms with purpose within His plan. Humanity knows of the reality that is the blue planet...there is more, much more.

But for today, know this...that the first step in the right direction *is still...the right step.* **Take the right step. Start now.** It is our hope that any that read these pages will be inspired to, at the very least, consider what has been written. What they do after that point, we hope, is to accept the invitation to greatness and become wisdom seekers! We Await you! Come join our forces of light bearers and bring radiance into your world, into the heart of the human Spirit! There are none to lose! Be vigilant! We are applauding all that would grow with us and make paradise prevail! Eons we wait for these moments. *Astara Highlands - so mote it be!*

ABOUT THE AUTHOR
PATRICIA LEAHY LINDSAY

Born in Sharon Hill, Pennsylvania on March 1, 1946, to James J. Leahy and Eleanor M. Leahy, who moved shortly after her birth to their favorite place on the Planet Earth, Avalon, New Jersey. Pat was a good student and exhibited talent in art, music, and business. She would be the first to tell you she cringed at Algebra and suffered through auto mechanics. Pat was a true artist preferring to swim, surf, and basically water ski though life with a smile. (She still swims and smiles.)

Patricia was a staff writer and recording artist for Jamie Records and Publishing Co., Philadelphia, Pennsylvania, formerly a member of "BMI" (Broadcast Music Inc.) and has owned and sold part of a small business prior to her marriage. DWELLERS ON TWO PLANES, a non-fictional work of metaphysical, uplifting, and inspirational intent, is Patricia's third book. DWELLERS ON TWO PLANES is a channeled book of "Spiritual guidance into the Millennium and beyond", written with her Spiritual guide, a teacher from the original order of priests-Melchizedek.

In 1989, Pat married a brilliant RF engineer, James E. Lindsay, living with him in New York, New Jersey, North Carolina, Georgia, and most recently in Tallassee, Alabama where she currently resides on five beautiful acres of fine Alabama soil.

Pat's husband James died in July 2005. It was after his death that Pat began writing with teacher Rama. Pat graduated her metaphysical study work in 1994, and is an 8th degree scholar.

Pat's first book, IT COMES DOWN TO WANTING SOMETHING and DESERT QUEEN, her second book, are available now for review and purchase on her website: patricialindsaybooks.com.

Peter Heberer,
Assistant Editor, Production Manager-
DWELLERS ON TWO PLANES

Printed in the United States
By Bookmasters